Dynamics of Income Distribution

Dynamics of
Income Distribution

JOHN CREEDY

Basil Blackwell

First published 1985

Basil Blackwell Ltd
108 Cowley Road, Oxford OX4 1JF, UK

Basil Blackwell Inc.
432 Park Avenue South, Suite 1505,
New York, NY 10016, USA

British Library Cataloguing in Publication Data
Creedy, John, 1949–
    Dynamics of income distribution.
    1. Income distribution – Mathematical models
    I. Title
    339.2'2'072   HB523
    ISBN 0-631-14499-4

Library of Congress Cataloging in Publication Data
Creedy, John, 1949–
    Dynamics of income distribution.
    Bibliography: p.
    Includes index
    1. Income distribution – Econometric models. 2. Income tax – Econometric models. I. Title
    HB523.C73 1985   339.2   85-6163
    ISBN 0-631-14499-4

Typeset by Unicus Graphics Ltd, Horsham
Printed in Great Britain by The Camelot Press Ltd, Southampton

Dedicated to the memory of Alan Brown

Contents

viii *Contents*

Preface

This book concentrates in a systematic form the main results of part of my work on income distribution. It is not however a simple collection of papers. In every case the material has been considerably reorganized, rewritten and reduced. Many derivations have been reduced or excluded, and a great deal of empirical work has been deleted from the original. In some cases additional material has been added. Reference to my own work has been completely avoided in the text, although of course cross references between chapters of this book are used. In the notes on further reading at the end of each chapter, the main sources and references to further extensions are given. The list of references at the end of the book cannot pretend to be even a partial bibliography of the subject; it could easily be multiplied many times. But it rapidly became clear that to refer to a wider range of literature would produce a list of disproportionate length.

Acknowledgements

My work on income distribution began in 1971 with the suggestion by Alan Brown that I might like to do some further work on a model of age–earnings profiles, mentioned briefly in Aitchison and Brown (1957) and in more detail in Brown (1967). This work developed into my B.Phil. Thesis on *Economic Cycles in the Lives of Individuals and Families* (1972), which in turn formed the basis of several later papers. Then from 1973 to 1978, at the University of Reading, I had the good fortune to be associated with Peter Hart. Over that period he provided invaluable guidance and encouragement. During a short period of research from 1977 to 1978 at the National Institute of Economic and Social Research, I benefited considerably from discussions with Sig Prais. I am very grateful indeed for their help, although none of these people can be held responsible for any of the shortcomings of this book. I also like to think that this work reflects an indirect stimulus provided by some of the earlier work of A. L. Bowley on the analysis of income distribution. In fact it is also easy to find Bowley 'links' with the Oxford Institute of Economics and Statistics (where my B.Phil. Thesis was written), the University of Reading, the NIESR, and finally with the University of Durham.

I should also like to thank Mark Casson for suggesting this book and for constructive criticism, Anders Klevmarken and Peter Hart for allowing me to use some results from our joint analyses of Swedish and UK data, and Norman Gemmell for allowing me to use our joint work in chapter 12. I am very grateful to Kathryn Cowton for superb typing. Acknowledgement must also be made to the editors and publishers of the following journals for permission to reproduce material: *Review of Income and Wealth, Economic Journal, Oxford Economic Papers, Oxford Bulletin of Economics and Statistics, Public Finance, Journal of Public Economics*, and *Journal of Economic Studies*.

Part I

Introduction

1

The Statics and Dynamics
of Earnings

In view of the very large number of ways in which the study of
income distribution can be approached, it seems useful to begin
this book by attempting to explain the general motivation behind
the various analyses contained in the following chapters. The basic
purpose of the book is to summarize attempts to develop statistical
models and methods of analysis of income distribution which are
useful in the further study of a wide range of economic issues.
Although the emphasis is therefore on methods of dealing with or
analysing income distributions, some examples of (and further
references to) applications are of course given. The breadth of
possible applications stems essentially from the important role of
income distribution in economics.

Now it is perfectly proper to argue that the distribution of
earnings, other sources of income and of wealth all arise as a result
of a very complex economic process involving many interdepen-
dencies among individuals. The generation process involves many
different types of choice (where objectives are multidimensional),
many different elements of chance, and many types of constraint
imposed on individuals and households. Despite the large extent
of endogeneity in practice, it is however necessary, if any progress
is to be made, to take problems 'one at a time'. It is argued here
that for many purposes the isolation and succinct description of
the types of statistical regularity presented below can thus be of
some value.

The Need for Dynamic Analyses

In any study involving the distribution of income it is of course
very important to pay serious attention to the following three

aspects. First there is the question of the precise concept of income used (usually defined with reference to the *source* of the flow); secondly there is the unit of analysis (whether individual, family or household); and thirdly there is the choice of appropriate time period of analysis. The general statement made in the first paragraph above can now be made somewhat more specific. A major motivation for many of the following analyses is the belief that a simple static description of income measured over a fairly short period rarely provides sufficient information. It is often required to describe directly the way in which incomes change over time and to be able to assess the effects of such mobility on incomes when measured over a much longer period.

Some examples of the relevance of the dynamics of earnings may be given very briefly here. There is a great deal of interest in the measurement of 'inequality' within specified populations, but very often only annual or even shorter term data are used. Attempts are often made to assess whether or not 'inequality' has increased or decreased over time, by simple comparative static analysis. However, individuals' relative income positions seldom remain unchanged over time; indeed many policies are designed to influence relative income status directly. An increase in a static, short term measure of inequality is in fact quite consistent with there having been a significant amount of 'egalitarian' mobility over time, to the extent that those in the lower deciles may on average have moved to higher positions. A society that has very little 'static inequality', relative to another society, may nevertheless allow so little mobility that a distribution of a long term measure of income would give quite a different impression.

It is often required, by policy makers and by individuals considering, for example, occupational choice, to make comparisons among occupations in terms of income prospects. Since there is in general a systematic variation in earnings with age, and as age distributions differ between industries, a simple comparison of average earnings measured over a short period will be of little value. Some occupations are characterized by greater instability of earnings from one year to the next, and this should be included explicitly in any comparison. Furthermore, many analyses of the way in which labour markets operate will be concerned with patterns of job mobility and career progression.

Occupational choice has already been mentioned, but of course many areas of behaviour have a life cycle aspect. The general importance of the life cycle in economics has often been stressed, and there is the considerable literature on 'life cycle' theories of consumption and saving behaviour. However, it is notable that in the best known studies of 'life cycle' savings, very little attention was actually given to the process of earnings changes over age. Highly aggregative time series models were often used, involving concepts such as 'expected future income', without serious discussion of the aggregation difficulties involved. Earnings dynamics are even relevant in the simple case in which all individuals are assumed to have linear consumption functions relating current consumption to current income. If the marginal propensities to consume differ among individuals, it can be shown that the aggregate marginal propensity will also reflect the nature of relative earnings movements, and the correlation between earnings mobility and individual propensities.

The analysis of government policy towards 'social insurance', covering unemployment, sickness and pensions, is another area that demands a longer term perspective, especially in terms of the distributional impact of such policies. Each policy involves redistribution between stages of the life cycle (from work to retirement, and from periods of work to periods of unemployment and sickness), as well as redistribution among individuals. Such redistribution among persons may be a deliberate feature of the policy, but it is very difficult indeed to assess its quantitative importance. However, it is only in recent years that more attention has come to be paid to the dynamics of these aspects of the labour market. The economic analysis of these issues involves many complexities, and simple models of earnings dynamics which can be conveniently integrated into larger analyses are therefore required.

It is useful at this stage to stress an important point concerning earnings dynamics, life cycle analyses and the availability of appropriate data. Despite the investment during more recent years in the collection of some longitudinal data, they are still something of a luxury. Data providing information about many individual characteristics over many years are still rare. The analyses presented below have an advantage in requiring relatively few data. There are, furthermore, contexts in which it would not even be possible to collect the full amount of data that might ideally be required. In investigating the possible effects of various social insurance policies on, say, lifetime earnings, or in comparing prospective lifetime earnings in various occupations for a series of cohorts entering the labour market, the relevant data could not be obtained even for straightforward comparisons. Thus the models, estimated from more limited data, must be capable of generating further results. For example, it is helpful if they can be used for simulation purposes in order to examine a range of policy alternatives. Similarly, it is helpful if a model of earnings dynamics, estimated from data covering a number of years, can be applied to a larger proportion of the life cycle, and has convenient aggregation properties.

Outline of the Book

Although each chapter is provided with an introduction placing the analysis in context, it seems useful here to make a few remarks about the general structure of the book, if only to stress what the book is *not* trying to do. Part II is taken up with discussion of two issues that at first sight may not seem to fit too well with the general emphasis of the book on dynamic aspects of income distribution. There is an enormous and growing literature concerned with the measurement of 'inequality', concentrating on conceptual issues of comparing 'static' distributions. The concept of inequality is of course far from simple, but this study really makes no attempt to examine the many issues, interesting and important as they are. It is concerned with the more practical and pragmatic problems of comparing distributions, and discussions of inequality are mainly limited to the use of statistical measures of dispersion. However, a criticism of a measure used extensively throughout this book, the variance of the logarithms, has been raised, suggesting that it does not even satisfy the very simple criterion that a transfer of income from rich to poor should decrease the measure of inequality. For this reason the criticism should be taken seriously, and forms the subject of chapter 2, where it is argued that the problem is of very minor practical importance.

There is a very long tradition of studies that are concerned with the question of the appropriate functional form to be used in describing income distributions. This subject has been linked with the analysis of so-called stochastic models of the 'genesis' of the income distribution. Such models are formulated in terms of a process of successive earnings changes involving stochastic or chance elements, and the resulting equilibrium distribution (that stable distribution that arises after the application of the stochastic process over a 'very long' period of change) is derived. It must be stressed that the present study, in which 'chance' earnings changes also play a large part, makes no attempt to contribute to this literature. The emphasis is on changes over the life cycle, and a labour force in which 'births' and 'deaths' play an important part. Equilibrium distributions have no place in this context. Although much use is made here of the lognormal distribution, whose detailed properties have been investigated by Aitchison and Brown (1957), no appeal is made to stochastic models that are capable of generating that distribution. Appeal is however made to its ability to describe many empirical frequency distributions closely over the whole range of income, and by its convenient analytical properties which make it so valuable when used as a component of larger models.

Many stochastic models have been produced to generate the Pareto distribution. It is therefore ironic that Pareto himself rejected stochastic models on the basis, it seems, of a narrow view of stochastic processes, limited to a simple binomial process which leads to a Normal distribution. Chapter 3 below may really be seen as an exercise in the history of economic, or econometric, thought which is concentrated on the question of functional form. In fact it is not difficult to produce a 'new' functional form to describe income distributions, and equally it is all too easy to reject nearly all functional forms on the basis of simple goodness of fit tests having fairly arbitrary loss functions (such as the χ^2 test, which with very large samples will reject virtually everything). It is shown in chapter 3 that Pareto's preferred functional form is rejected by his own data in favour of a generalization that he suggested and then rejected.

Part III turns to the main theme, that of earnings dynamics, and considers alternative specifications of the process of relative earnings changes. Chapter 4 examines models based on standard regression analysis, and chapter 5 turns to the use of matrices in the same context. This Part is concerned with *relative* earnings changes of a constant group of individuals of the same age; that is, belonging to the same birth cohort. The regression models are restricted to those in which all individuals have the same parameters, since the available data are limited to a small number of time periods.

Part IV then examines the more systematic changes in earnings associated with ageing, and combines the results with those of chapter 4 to produce a simple model (involving only five parameters) which is capable of describing the changing distribution of earnings for a wide range of occupations. In examining such earnings changes there is of course the well known identification problem arising from the fact that the average earnings of a cohort may change for several reasons. These include the possible influence of calendar time which may affect all groups, the general influence of ageing and changes associated with each specific cohort. The influence of ageing alone can only be estimated after making strong *a priori* assumptions about the 'time' and 'cohort' effects. This identification problem arises both with cross sectional *and* longitudinal data. The use of alternative restrictions is considered briefly in chapter 6, which then goes on to illustrate how the basic model can be adjusted to allow for differing household composition and can be integrated into models of occupational choice and consumption. While this chapter produces a conditional distribution of earnings for each age group, chapter 7 goes on to examine the problem of obtaining the aggregate distribution, over all age groups combined. It seems that this question has received little attention, other than in the study by Rutherford (1955), who examined a very simple age–earnings profile and an exponential age distribution. Chapter 7 uses a wider range of earnings profiles and age distributions, and shows the conditions under which the marginal earnings distribution deviates from lognormality even when all the conditional distributions are lognormal.

Part V then turns to a rather different problem of aggregation, that of adding together the earnings of a number of consecutive years. Chapter 8 obtains some basic results concerning the dispersion of the sum of several years' earnings, and chapter 9 then examines the distribution of lifetime earnings. The latter chapter compares alternative measures of the level of lifetime earnings in different occupations, as well as obtaining the coefficient of variation of lifetime earnings under alternative assumptions about the process of earnings mobility. A simulation procedure for producing a set of individual age–earnings profiles is then presented and used.

Part VI then considers some aspects of earnings changes in the context of income taxation. Chapter 10, continuing the theme of the previous Part, compares a system of income taxation based on annual income with one based on an average of three years' income. Chapter 11 provides convenient analytical results for a number of systems of income tax and transfer payments, concerning the relationships between tax rates and levels of benefits and the effect on a measure of dispersion of incomes. The effect on total revenue, within a progressive tax system, of a general increase in money incomes which is not matched by a similar increase in tax thresholds is then treated in chapter 12.

Further Reading

For a general discussion of static and dynamic aspects of income distribution see Hart (1981). Good examples of empirical studies which stressed the importance of life cycle factors are Fisher (1952) for the United States and Lydall (1955, 1955a) for Britain. Stochastic processes for the size distribution of incomes are examined in Klein (1962), Hart (1973), Shorrocks (1975) and Ord (1975), with a useful general discussion of their development in Brown (1976). Further discussion of criteria for descriptions of income distribution can be found in Aitchison and Brown (1954, 1957). Comparisons of functional forms are far too numerous to mention here, but Salem and Mount (1974) and Singh and Maddala (1976) provide two interesting examples.

Part II

Dispersion and Functional form

2

The Principle of Transfers and the Variance of Logarithms

2.1 The Principle of Transfers

In his book on the inequality of incomes, Dalton (1929) provided a substantial contribution to the economic analysis of inequality, following in the spirit of Cannan (1914). Despite the breadth of Dalton's approach, his work is probably now best remembered for its technical discussion of the measurement of inequality, first published in 1920 and included as an appendix to his book. The two main features, which received considerable attention in the late 1960s and early 1970s, are his emphasis on *welfare* comparisons (rather than income comparisons) and his investigation of alternative measures of inequality according to their ability to satisfy a set of basic criteria.

Dalton began by considering the situation where 'the economic welfare of different persons is additive, [and] the relation of income to economic welfare is the same for all members of the community' (1929, Appendix, p. 2). If $U(y)$ represents the utility function, and the distribution function of incomes is given by $F(y)$, then total welfare, W, is written as

$$W = \int U(y) \, dF(y) \tag{2.1}$$

If there is diminishing marginal utility, then it follows that W is maximized with complete equality of y. Dalton was thereby led to suggest that 'the inequality of any given distribution may conveniently be defined as the ratio of the total economic welfare attainable under an equal distribution to the total economic welfare attained under the given distribution' (1929, p. 2). In the equal distribution case all individuals would receive the arithmetic mean, $E(y)$, so Dalton's measure, D_1, is

$$D_1 = U(E(y)) \Big/ \int U(y) \, \mathrm{d}F(y) \tag{2.2}$$

The form of the measure chosen in practice therefore depends explicitly on the functional form assumed for $U(y)$.

One of Dalton's criteria for assessing inequality measures has come to be known as the 'Principle of Transfers'. He suggested that 'if there are only two income receivers, and a transfer of income takes place from the richer to the poorer, inequality is diminished', so long as their *relative* positions (ranking) in the distribution remain unchanged. Then 'In comparing the distributions, in which the total income and the number of income receivers are the same, ... one might be able to be evolved by the other by means of a series of transfers of this kind. In such a case we would say with certainty that the inequality of one was less than that of the other' (1929, p. 5). Dalton did not however investigate the implications of his principle at length.

Both of these aspects of Dalton's work were taken up in the well known paper by Atkinson (1970). First, Atkinson rejected Dalton's measure (2.2) on the grounds that it was not invariant with respect to monotonic transformations of $U(y)$. In this connection Atkinson preferred to substitute a 'social welfare function' for the cardinal utility function. To overcome the problem, Atkinson introduced the concept of the 'equally distributed equivalent' level of income per head, y_e, defined as that level of income that, if equally distributed, would produce the same welfare as the actual distribution:

$$U(y_e) = \int U(y) \, \mathrm{d}F(y) \tag{2.3}$$

and defined a new class of measures, I, based on

$$I = 1 - y_e / E(y) \tag{2.4}$$

The value of y_e clearly depends on the form chosen for the social welfare function; for example in the logarithmic case it is the geometric mean income. The inequality measures defined by (2.4) can in fact be seen to depend on a ratio of two measures of location of the existing distribution.

The second aspect of Dalton's work taken up by Atkinson concerned the Principle of Transfers. He examined the close relationship between the welfare rankings (for concave functions U) of distributions, and the rankings according to the Lorenz measure. In the latter case, one distribution is unambiguously more unequal than another if the Lorenz curve of the first lies outside that of the second distribution. The Principle of Transfers was shown to be equivalent to the concept of the 'mean preserving spread' introduced by Rothschild and Stiglitz (1971) in their analysis of increasing risk. Atkinson's use of mean preserving spreads in connection with the Principle of Transfers stimulated a great deal of analysis of the relationships between alternative criteria according to which distributions are judged to have become more (or less) equal. This work has also helped to make explicit the 'welfare' implications of various statistical measures of inequality. More general results were obtained by Dasgupta *et al.* (1973), who explored the relations between the Lorenz measure, Dalton's Principle of Transfers, and a social welfare function defined over individual incomes and according to which distributions are ranked. They showed that for any social welfare function U, which is not necessarily additive and which need only be S-concave, if the Lorenz curve for one distribution, y, lies entirely inside that of any other distribution x, then $U(y) > U(x)$ and the rankings are equivalent (Dasgupta *et al.*, 1973, p. 182; Sen, 1973, p. 54). S-concavity is weaker than both concavity (which requires $tU(x) + (1-t)U(y) < U\{tx + (1-t)y\}$; $0 < t < 1$) and quasi-concavity (requiring $\min\{U(x), U(y)\} < U\{tx + (1-t)y\}$; $0 < t < 1$). The function U is S-concave if for all doubly stochastic matrices Q (all entries >0 and all row and column sums equal unity); $U(Qx) > U(x)$.

Because of the highly general nature of these results and the assumptions underlying them, it would seem that any measure of inequality of income whose 'corresponding' welfare function is not strictly S-concave is an unacceptable measure. The discovery of the equivalence of rankings according to Lorenz measures, (S-concave) welfare measures and the Principle of Transfers did indeed lead to wide criticisms of any measure that did not satisfy the Principle of Transfers. One such measure is the variance of logarithms. Thus, while Sen regards the fact that this measure is more sensitive to transfers at lower than at higher incomes as a point in its favour, he adds 'the fact that the standard deviation of logarithms does not even satisfy ... [the Principle of Transfers] ... may appear to be, in some sense, much more clearly objectionable' (1973, p. 34). This comment implies strong criticism, although the use of the words 'may appear' and 'in some sense' do not really provide a sufficient indication of the extent to which σ^2 is in fact 'objectionable'. The purpose of this chapter is therefore to assess this criticism in more detail. This is required because the variance of logarithms is used extensively in this book and has a number of well known properties which are extremely useful for empirical work. In particular the decomposition of the logarithmic variance is much more convenient than the decomposition of other measures. Even more important is the fact that it can be extended to cover dynamic components of changes in income distribution.

In order to assess the criticism that the variance of the logarithms violates the Principle of Transfers, it is first necessary to provide a convenient decomposition, as presented in section 2.2. Section 2.3 then investigates the range of situations under which the Principle is violated. Finally section 2.4 briefly considers the empirical relevance of the criticisms.

2.2   A Decomposition of the Variance of Logarithms

Before considering the problem in more detail it is first worth stressing that if the income distribution can be described by the two-parameter lognormal distribution $\Lambda(y \mid \mu, \sigma^2)$, where μ and σ^2 are respectively the mean and variance of the logarithms of income, then there is in fact no problem. This point is clear from the demonstration by Aitchison and Brown (1957, p. 113) that Lorenz curves for two-parameter lognormal distributions cannot intersect, and are also symmetric. In addition, consider the iso-elastic welfare function used by Atkinson (1970), and given by,

$$U(y) = a + \{b/(1-\epsilon)\}y^{1-\epsilon} \qquad \epsilon \neq 1 \qquad \text{- (2.5)}$$

where ϵ is referred to as the 'inequality aversion' parameter. The value of I (after substitution into (2.4)) can be shown to be equal to

$$I = 1 - \exp(-\epsilon\sigma^2/2) \qquad (2.6)$$

and depends in a simple way on the variance of logarithms. However, in practice the lognormal can be regarded as only an approximation to the income distribution, even where the statistical fit is quite good, and of course no single functional form can be expected to be appropriate in all circumstances.

In examining the behaviour of inequality measures in response to income transfers it was usual to consider only very small transfers. For example Marfels (1972) approximates the inequality measure by a Taylor series, so if the initial distribution $y = (p_1, \dots, p_i, \dots, p_k, \dots)$, for $p_i > 0$, $\Sigma p_i = 1$, is changed by an amount $\Delta y = (0, \dots, +\epsilon, 0, \dots, -\epsilon, \dots)$ then the change in an inequality measure $I(y)$ is given by $I(y + \Delta y) - I(y) = \Sigma \Delta y_i(\partial I/\partial y_i) = \epsilon(\partial I/\partial p_j - \partial I/\partial p_i)$. Marfels did not consider the variance of the logarithms although the same method has been applied by others. However, it seems intuitively obvious that whether or not the principle is violated will depend on the actual size of the transfer. The effect on σ^2 of discrete transfers can be analysed as follows.

Consider two samples of size n_1 and n_2 with means and variances of logarithms μ_1, μ_2 and σ_1^2, σ_2^2 respectively, and let $w_i = n_i/(n_1 + n_2)$. The variance of the logarithms of the two samples combined, σ^2, is

$$\sigma^2 = w_1(\sigma_1^2 + \mu_1^2) + w_2(\sigma_2^2 + \mu_2^2) - (w_1\mu_1 + w_2\mu_2)^2 \qquad (2.7)$$

Since in general the average of squared deviations about the origin is equal to the sum of the square of the mean and the average squared deviations about the mean. This can be rewritten as

$$\sigma^2 = w_1\sigma_1^2 + w_2\sigma_2^2 + w_1 w_2(\mu_1 - \mu_2)^2 \qquad (2.8)$$

If a transfer within the second sample takes place, then where the new mean and variance of the logarithms after the transfer are μ_2^* and σ_2^{*2} respectively, the change in the variance of the combination, $\Delta\sigma^2$, is given by

$$\Delta\sigma^2/w_2 = (\sigma_2^2 - \sigma_2^{*2}) + w_1(\mu_2^2 - \mu_2^{*2}) - 2w_1\mu_1(\mu_2 - \mu_2^*) \quad (2.9)$$

If, further, n_2 is no larger than 2 and if n_1 is large, then $w_1 \simeq 1$ and $w_1 w_2 \simeq w_2 = w$, say. Thus (2.9) can be rewritten as

$$\Delta\sigma^2/w = (\sigma_2^{*2} + \mu_2^{*2}) - (\sigma_2^2 + \mu_2^2) - 2\mu_1(\mu_2^* - \mu_2^*) \qquad (2.10)$$

2.3 The Type and Size of Transfer

Consider a transfer of δ from person B, say, with income X_B to person A with income X_A (where $X_B < X_A$). Then making the appropriate substitutions in (2.10) gives

$$\Delta\sigma^2/w = \tfrac{1}{2}[\{\log(X_A + \delta)\}^2 + \{\log(X_B - \delta)\}^2 - (\log X_A)^2$$
$$- (\log X_B)^2] - 2\mu_1\{\tfrac{1}{2}\log(X_A + \delta) + \log(X_B - \delta)$$
$$- \log X_A - \log X_B\}$$

which can be simplified to give

$$2\Delta\sigma^2/w = \log\left(1 + \frac{\delta}{X_A}\right)\log\frac{X_A(X_A + \delta)}{m^2} + \log\left(1 - \frac{\delta}{X_B}\right)$$

$$\times \log\frac{X_B(X_B - \delta)}{m^2} \tag{2.11}$$

where m is the geometric mean income in the sample of size n_1. For $X_A > m$ the first term in (2.11) is always positive, and for $X_B < m$ the second term is always positive. Thus transfers *across the geometric mean* always increase the variance of the logs. If both A and B have incomes below the geometric mean, then $X_B < X_A < m$ and therefore $|\log(X_A/m)| < |\log(X_B/m)|$. Furthermore $|\log(1 + \delta/X_A)| < |\log(1 - \delta/X_B)|$. Given these two inequalities it can be seen that even when the first term in (2.11) is negative when $X_A < m$ (it may actually be positive depending on the size of δ), the size of the second term (which is positive) is always larger in absolute terms; thus the value of σ^2 always increases. Hence σ^2 does not violate the Principle of Transfers for transfers taking place *below the geometric mean*.

The case where $X_A > X_B > m$ is not so clear, since the transfer will only unequivocally increase σ^2 if

$$\frac{\delta}{m} > \frac{k_B^2 - 1}{k_B} \qquad \text{where } k_B = \frac{X_B}{m} > 1 \tag{2.12}$$

Person B will always be able to afford such a transfer, however. To examine this case further it is useful to define the following terms:

$$\theta_B = \delta/X_B \qquad \text{and} \qquad \theta_A = \delta/X_A \qquad \text{with} \qquad \psi = k_B/k_A < 1$$

Using this notation, (2.11) can be simplified to give

$$2\Delta\sigma^2/w = \log(k_B^2/\psi^2)\log(1 + \theta_B\psi) + \log k_B^2 \log(1 - \theta_B)$$

$$+ \{\log(1 + \theta_B\psi)\}^2 + \{\log(1 - \theta_B)\}^2 \tag{2.13}$$

Changes in σ^2 can then be examined by considering variations in the relative values of only θ_B, ψ and k_B; with $\theta_B < 1$ and $\psi < 1$. ($k_B > 1$ for transfers above the geometric mean.) For given values of θ_B, the proportion of B's income transferred, it is possible to calculate the values of k_B and ψ for which σ^2 begins to violate the Principle of Transfers. It may be thought that equation (2.13) can be simplified by expanding the logarithmic series and neglecting terms with powers of θ_B greater than two. However, the expansions converge very slowly, so much higher powers of θ_B must be retained. Dalton himself noted a similar case where Pigou had neglected higher terms in a Taylor expansion when considering the coefficient of variation. See Dalton (1929, Appendix, p. 9, n. 1) and Pigou's later acknowledgement of this point in Pigou (1952, p. 97).

Some examples of combinations that violate the Principle of Transfers are shown in figure 2.1. The vertical axis shows the ratio of transferor's to transferee's income, and the horizontal axis shows the ratio of transferor's income to the geometric mean. Each profile in the figure is drawn for a different value of the ratio of the size of the transfer to the transferor's income. Combinations of ψ and k_B to the bottom right of each profile lead to violation of the Principle of Transfers. Thus for each combination in that area, a transfer of specified size from one person to another, relatively richer, person (where both are above the geometric mean) will cause the variance of the logarithms of income to *decrease*, rather than increase. These examples indicate three general features of those cases that lead to perverse results. The Principle is more likely to be violated:

1   the smaller the transfer as a proportion of the transferor's income;

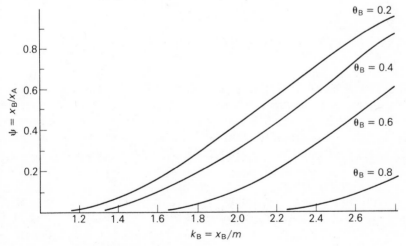

Figure 2.1   The Principle of Transfers.

2   for any given transfer, the larger the ratio of the transferor's income to the geometric mean;
3   for any given transfer, the larger the initial relative difference between the two people's incomes.

Equation (2.13) can also be used to examine the taxonomy of inter-regional transfers; for example, the conditions under which a transfer from someone in one region to a richer person in another region would increase the 'inequality' of one distribution relative to the other. Thus if only one person's income increases by the amount δ, then the second group can be ignored and σ_2^{*2} and σ_2^2 are set to zero.

Substitution into (2.13) gives, after rearrangement,

$$\Delta \sigma^2/w = \log(1 + \delta/x) \log\{(1 + \delta/x) x^2/m^2\} \qquad (2.14)$$

This shows that if someone with income above the geometric mean receives an increase ($x > m$, $\delta > 0$), and if someone below the geometric mean is the transferor ($x < m$, $\delta < 0$), then the variance of the logarithm always increases. Other alternatives are more equivocal. If the transferee is below the geometric mean ($x/m = k < 1$, $\delta > 0$), it can be seen that σ^2 *decreases* if $(\delta/m) < (1 - k^2)/k$. On the other hand, if the transferor is above the geometric mean ($k > 1$, $\delta < 0$), σ^2 will decrease if $|\delta/m| < (k^2 - 1)/k$. In the latter case the additional condition $\delta/m < k$ must be imposed in order to ensure that the transferor can afford to make the necessary transfer.

2.4   The Relevance of Possible Violations

These results indicate the range of situations in which violation of the Principle of Transfers is *possible*, but it is also necessary to consider the *probability* of transfers taking place within the relevant range. However, it is not possible to obtain the actual probability of such transfers taking place without at the same time providing an explicit treatment of changes in relative earnings. This aspect is usually neglected by those criticizing the use of the variance of logarithms on these grounds, because of the emphasis on static measures of inequality. Remaining within the static framework it is however possible to obtain some idea of an *upper limit* to the probability of perverse transfers taking place, depending on the distribution of income before the transfer takes place.

It is instructive to translate some of the information in figure 2.1 into standardized form in the logarithms. Thus if X has a geometric mean m and variance of the logarithms σ^2, then the corresponding standardized variable Z (which has zero mean and unit variance) is given by $(\log X - \log m)/\sigma = \{\log(X/m)\}/\sigma$. For any value of X_B/m it is possible to express the minimum value of the income of the transferee, X_A, required to violate the Principle of Transfers, in standardized form. This is done using the result that violation of the Principle requires $X_A > X_B/\psi$, so $Z_A = \{\log(X_A/m)\}/\sigma = \{\log(X_B/m) - \log \psi\}/\sigma$. The appropriate value of ψ for each X_B/m is obtained from figure 2.1. Some results, for different values of X_B/m, and for two different values of θ_B and of σ^2, are given in table 2.1. It should be noted that the value of 0.5 for σ^2 ($\sigma = 0.707$) is higher than the values usually obtained for empirical income distributions, other than perhaps for data presented in highly aggregative form. It can be seen that the values of Z_A and Z_B are quite high, especially for the lower σ and higher θ_B. For example, consider a person B whose income is double the geometric mean (that is, $X_B/m = 2$), and who transfers 20 per cent of that income to person A ($\theta_B = 0.2$). Table 2.1 shows that if the pre-transfer standard deviation of logarithms is 0.447, then B's log-income is 1.55 standard deviations from the mean of logs, and for the Principle of Transfers to be violated the transferee must have a log-income at least 3.47 standard deviations from the logarithmic mean.

This information in table 2.1 can then be used to obtain an upper limit to the conditional probability that a person with income X_B transfers a proportion θ_B of that income to another person with income X_A, such that the Principle of Transfers is violated. If the pre-transfer distribution function of income is $F(X)$, which will not of course hold after the transfer, this conditional probability is simply $\{1 - F(X_A)\}$. The product of this value and the ordinate $f(X_B)$ may be regarded as an upper limit to the joint 'probability' that a person selected at random will have an income in the range $X_B + dx$ *and* make a violating transfer.

This can be carried out, for all alternatives in table 2.1, for any form of $F(X)$. For the convenient case of lognormality, the highest values of $f(X_B)\{1 - F(X_A)\}$ are found to be less than 1 per cent, and most are negligible. When it is remembered that this is strictly an upper limit, and that in practice the lognormal distribution overstates the proportions in the upper tail, the argument against the use of σ^2 is hardly significant.

Table 2.1 Standardized values for principle of transfers

| X_B/m | ψ | | $Z_B = \log(X_B/m)/\sigma$ | | $Z_A = \{\log(X_B/m) - \log\psi\}/\sigma$ | | | |
| | | | | | $\sigma = 0.447$ | | $\sigma = 0.707$ | |
	$\theta_B = 0.2$	$\theta_B = 0.6$	$\sigma = 0.447$	$\sigma = 0.707$	$\theta_B = 0.2$	$\theta_B = 0.6$	$\theta_B = 0.2$	$\theta_B = 0.6$
1.4	0.07	—	0.75	0.48	6.55	—	4.14	—
1.6	0.17	—	1.05	0.67	5.01	—	3.17	—
1.8	0.29	0.05	1.32	0.83	4.08	8.02	2.58	5.07
2.0	0.43	0.10	1.55	0.98	3.47	6.70	2.19	4.24
2.2	0.57	0.20	1.76	1.12	3.02	5.37	1.91	3.39
2.4	0.69	0.33	1.96	1.24	2.79	4.44	1.76	2.81
2.6	0.85	0.47	2.14	1.35	2.50	3.83	1.58	2.42
2.8	0.95	0.60	2.30	1.46	2.41	3.45	1.53	2.18

It is therefore suggested that the fact that the variance of logarithms *can* violate the Principle of Transfers need be regarded as no more than a *curiosum*. The applied economist can therefore safely take advantage of the other extremely convenient properties of this measure.

Further Reading

This chapter is based on Creedy (1977a). The literature on inequality measurement is too great to be mentioned here,but a useful bibliography is given by Atkinson (1983), following the reprinting of his 1970 paper. Some of the criticism of the variance of logarithms has come from those interested in measuring business concentration, where the variance is much larger than that usually observed for income data. For discussion and further references to the debate see Hart (1978, 1980, 1982a). A useful comparison of inequality measures is also contained in Hart (1978). Cases where the variance of logarithms behaves in a perverse manner have of course been observed; see Creedy and Gemmell (1984) in the context of incomes and Hart (1982) in the context of the size of trade unions.

3

Pareto and the Distribution of Income

Pareto's first substantial work in economics, published in 1896 at the age of 48, was his short paper on *'La Courbe de la Repartition de la Richesse'*. This paper presented his now famous 'Pareto distribution' of income, and is often cited as a pioneering example of applied econometric research. The major empirical result obtained by Pareto, after estimating the parameters of his formula describing the distribution of income for a wide variety of places and times, was that the distribution displayed considerable stability. A great deal of emphasis was placed on this result; indeed, the distribution was for many years referred to as 'Pareto's *law*'. A great deal of energy has been devoted to the development of theoretical models of income distribution that are capable of producing a Pareto distribution; examples include Champernowne (1953), Mandelbrot (1960), Steindl (1965) and Lydall (1968), although the latter's hierarchical model is very different in approach from the earlier 'stochastic' models. The formula was used extensively for interpolation purposes by the Inland Revenue, and was even used (successfully) to stimulate a more intensive search for tax evaders by Josiah Stamp. A situation in fact existed where for many years statisticians were estimating functional forms for income distribution, using official data that had been 'smoothed' using the Pareto 'law'.

Pareto did not himself produce a model of the 'genesis' of his distribution, but the observed regularity of the functional form and the stability of the parameter governing the dispersion of incomes led him to make two strong conclusions. The first was that the distribution of income does not depend on chance or stochastic factors. This did not of course mean that there were not important changes in relative earnings over time within the distribution. Indeed, much of his *Traite* was concerned with the circulation of elites, and he stated in the *Manuel* (1909, p. 386) that 'la partie intérieure est ... en perpétuel movement; tandis que certains individus montent les régions supérieurs, d'autres en descendent'. Parento's view of 'chance', as shown in the long footnote in the *Cours* (1897, pp. 316–17), seems however to have been limited to a simple binomial process, and a consequent comparison with the upper tail of the Normal distribution. It is nevertheless true that many functional forms can be generated by a number of stochastic models of genesis of income distribution. Hence Pareto's argument was neatly dismissed by Gibrat (1931, p. 193): 'Pareto éliminait le hasard sous le prétext que sa formule différait de la formule de Gauss. Démonstration sans valeur, car le 'hasard' peut donner naissance a des repartitions très différent de celle de la courbe en cloche. Les répartitions normales sont l'exception.' And later in a footnote Gibrat stated 'Il ne faut pas oublier que l'on peut toujours trouver un changement de variable tel que la courbe en cloche devienne une courbe quelconque donée à l'avance.' In view of his general approach, it may well be thought that Pareto would have rejected 'chance' factors even if his observed distribution had followed the Normal form.

Pareto's second argument, based on his observed stability, was that any artificial attempts to alter the distribution would be futile. This view was also dominant in the contemporary writings of the Social Darwinists. For example, only a year after the publication of Pareto's paper Spencer wrote (1897, p. 260) 'What can be more extreme absurdity than that of proposing to improve social life by breaking the fundamental law of social life?' Although Pareto later modified the extreme form of his first statements, he still seemed to regard his 'law' as fundamental. Thus in the *Manuel* (1909, p. 388) he suggested that 'si la constitution sociale venait a changer d'une facon radicale ... il semble difficile qu'il ait plus de hiérarchie, et la forme de cette hiérarchie pourrait entre semblable à cette qui nous est donnée par les revenues des invidus, mais elle ne correspondrait pas à des revenue en argent.'

The observed stability of the income distribution, also stressed by many subsequent investigators, raises important and wide ranging questions, and it would be extreme to dismiss the observation as mere 'coincidence'. Yet Pareto's statement, in the absence of a wider model of the generation of incomes, is not a valid inference, and provides an example of what Schumpeter (1968,

p. 112) had in mind when he wrote of Pareto that 'into everything that was not a theorem in the pure logic of economics the whole man and all the forces that conditioned him entered so unmistakably that it is more necessary than it usually is in an appraisal of scientific performance to convey an idea of that man and of those forces.'

The purpose of this chapter is *not* however to examine these aspects of Pareto's work in more detail, but to look more closely at some of the statistical issues raised by his analysis. To what extent are Pareto's statements consistent with the data that he published? A number of results were reported briefly by Pareto, but not reproduced in any of his published work. The chapter also examines the validity of those statements. The starting point is the reminder, by Brown (1976), that Pareto actually suggested a much more general functional form of the 'courbe des revenus', but then dismissed it fairly quickly. Section 3.1 considers this more general form and Pareto's discussion of it. Section 3.2 then presents maximum likelihood estimates of the general form, using the original data. This closer examination of Pareto's work seems justified in view of the fact that his results have been quoted so often in the literature, and the distribution bearing his name has been used so extensively.

3.1   The General Pareto Distribution

The best known form of Pareto's 'law' is expressed by the equation

$$\log N = \log K - \alpha \log x \tag{3.1}$$

where x denotes the level of income, N is the number of people with incomes equal to or greater than x, and K and α are parameters. The latter is of course independent of the units in which income is measured. In terms of the distribution function of income, $F(x)$, equation (3.1) can be rewritten as

$$\log\{1 - F(x)\} = \log A - \alpha \log x \tag{3.2}$$

Note that the intercept changes because $1 - F(x)$ represents the *proportion*, while N is the absolute number, of incomes above or equal to x. It is convenient to write $\log A = \alpha \log x_0$, where x_0 is now the 'threshold' income level. Then

$$F(x) = 1 - (x_0/x)^\alpha \tag{3.3}$$

and the use of α as a measure of inequality depends on the assumption that x_0 remains constant. Pareto did not himself use α to measure inequality; see Pareto (1909, p. 320).

After presenting the log–linear form, Pareto noted a certain amount of concavity when values of $\log N$ were plotted against $\log x$, and suggested 'une seconde approximation du phénomène' (1896, p. 3). This was the four-parameter form

$$\log N = \log A - \alpha \log(x + \theta) - \beta x \qquad (3.4)$$

He went on to state that 'C'est probablement la forme générale des courbes de distribution' (1896, p. 3). Nevertheless Pareto only gave one set of estimates of the parameters of (3.4). These were for the Grand Duché d'Oldenbourg in 1890, and the following result was reported:

$$\log N = 8.72204 - 1.465 \log(x + 220) - 0.0000274x \qquad (3.5)$$

Pareto then remarked 'Pour d'autres pays, on a des valeurs de θ et β, encore plus petites et qui, en bien case paraissent être d'un ordre grandeur inférieur à celui des erreurs d'observation' (1896, p. 3). He consequently rejected this functional form in favour of his initial log–linear form.

This seems rather unusual when it is realized that the values of β and θ are not invariant with respect to the units of measurement, and that β is likely to be very small since the units of x are large and are elsewhere transformed by taking logarithms. Furthermore, it is of interest to note a point, made later by Pareto concerning estimation, that 'Il ne fait pas poursuivre une precision illusoire, et calculer laborieusement un grand nombre de decimales, qui, a fond, ne signifient rien du tout' (1906, p. 78). Yet Pareto presented his only reported value of β to seven decimal places. In fact ordinary least squares estimates of the slightly more simplified form $\log N = \log A - \alpha \log x - \beta x$, using Pareto's data, show that only 2 out of 17 values of β were not significantly different from zero. Furthermore 5 cases produce estimates of β that are larger than that obtained for Oldenbourg. This is far from consistent with Pareto's statement.

Pareto did however seem to attach more importance to the parameter θ. The inclusion of θ has the convenient effect of making the curve cut the N axis rather than approaching it asymptotically. Pareto reported that after examining distributions of different countries and sources of income 'la constant θ est negative, quand il s'agit du produit du travail; elle est positive quand il s'agit de la répartition de la fortune; elle est nulle, ou généralement assez petite, quand il s'agit du revenue totaux' (1897, p. 310). This is the interesting proposition that θ depends on the source of income. But no values of θ were reported, and Pareto did not consider how a distribution of total income with zero θ could be produced by some combination of separate distributions of 'profits' and 'wages'. Furthermore it is not clear how such a combination could give rise to even a 'Pareto' distribution. Consider for example the convolution of two Pareto variates x and y, where

$$x \text{ is } F_1(x \,|\, \alpha_1, x_0, \theta_1) \qquad \text{and} \qquad y \text{ is } F_2(y \,|\, \alpha_2, y_0, \theta_2)$$

Then the distribution function of $z = x + y$ is given by

$$F(z) = \int F_1(z - y)\, \mathrm{d}F_2(y)\, \mathrm{d}y \tag{3.6}$$

where integration is over the range of y. Substitution for F_1 and F_2 does not give a tractable expression that produces an $F(z)$ of Pareto's general form.

The 'general form' of Pareto's equation is of course non-linear in the parameters. Its estimation would have presented severe numerical difficulties for Pareto, and it is rather surprising that although he claimed to have obtained many estimates no explanation was given of the method of estimation used in the case of the single set of results presented for Oldenbourg. In estimating the two-parameter form Pareto explicitly rejected the use of ordinary least squares on the grounds that it was too laborious. The next section provides a convenient iterative method for the 'general form'. But first it is useful to note that this method is more widely applicable, as shown in the following subsection.

Further Analysis of the General Distribution

The first point to note about the general form in equation (3.4), without the term $-\beta x$, is that it is actually one of Pearson's well known class of distributions. It is a Pearson Type X1 distribution. An interesting feature is that the distribution can be shown to arise as a result of aggregating over a set of exponential distributions, where the exponential parameter itself follows the Gamma distribution; see Johnson and Kotz (1970, p. 233). This result is appropriate in, for example, situations of labour turnover in heterogeneous populations. If the probability of leaving a particular state is constant for each individual, then the distribution of the time spent in the state, $s(t)$, is exponential. Thus

$$s(t) = \alpha \mathrm{e}^{-\alpha t} \tag{3.7}$$

Suppose that α in turn follows a Gamma distribution with parameters λ and τ. The form of the distribution, $g(\alpha)$, is given by

$$g(\alpha) = \lambda^\tau \, e^{\tau-1} \, e^{-\lambda\alpha}/\Gamma(\tau) \tag{3.8}$$

with

$$\Gamma(\tau) = \int x^{\tau-1} \, e^{-x} \, dx = (\tau-1)\,\Gamma(\tau-1) = (\tau-1)!$$

The aggregate distribution of the time spent in the state, $f(t)$, is therefore given by

$$f(t) = \int s(t)\,g(\alpha)\,d\alpha \tag{3.9}$$

The substitution of (3.7) and (3.8) into (3.9) gives, after integration

$$f(t) = \frac{\tau}{\lambda}\left(\frac{\lambda}{\lambda+t}\right)^{\tau+1} \tag{3.10}$$

from which it can be seen that the proportion of individuals remaining in the state for longer than t periods is given by

$$1 - F(t) = \{\lambda/(\lambda+t)\}^\tau \tag{3.11}$$

This raises precisely the same estimation problem as the general Pareto form discussed above. The result has been used by Salant (1977) to examine the distribution of the time spent in unemployment, although Salent's calculations were obtained by 'computerized groping'.

It may also be noted that in demand studies, the use of double-logarithmic functions is quite common, although no intercept exists on the demand axis. This may sometimes be inconvenient, although the specification in (3.4), again with $-\beta x$ omitted, can easily be used. For an example in the context of the demand for recreational facilities, see Cheshire and Stabler (1976), who relate the visitor rate to the distance travelled.

3.2 Estimation and Results

Consider the estimation of the parameters a, α and θ of

$$\log N_i = a - \alpha \log(x_i + \theta) + u_i \tag{3.12}$$

from a sample of T observations. On the assumption that the u_i are independently normally distributed as $N(0, \sigma^2)$, the log-likelihood of the sample is given by

$$2 \log L = - T \log 2\pi - T \log \sigma^2 - \sum_{i=1}^{T} u_i^2/\sigma^2 \qquad (3.13)$$

When (3.12) refers to cumulative frequencies, the assumption of independence will not strictly hold, although it is used in what follows.

Setting the first derivatives of (3.13) to zero gives a set of four simultaneous non-linear equations. These can be solved most conveniently using Fisher's 'Method of Scoring'. This is essentially Newton's method, except that the second derivatives are replaced by their negative expectations. The 'scoring equations' are

$$\left[-E\left(\frac{\mathrm{d}^2 \log L}{\mathrm{d}p_i\,\mathrm{d}p_j} \right) \right][^{j+1}p_i - {}^j p_i] = \left[\frac{\mathrm{d} \log L}{\mathrm{d}p_i} \right] \qquad (3.14)$$

where ${}^j p_i$ is the estimate of the ith parameter p_i in the jth iteration. The vector of first derivatives on the right-hand side of (3.14) is the vector of 'Efficient Scores', while the matrix of negative expectations of second derivatives is the 'Information Matrix'. The inverse of this matrix in the last iteration is the variance/covariance matrix of the parameter estimates. All values are calculated using the estimates of p_i in the jth iteration. Using the fact that the mean and variance in Normal populations are independent, the information matrix can be partitioned, and the appropriate scoring equations for the parameters a, α and θ can be obtained as

$$\begin{bmatrix} T & -\Sigma \log y & -\alpha\Sigma(1/y) \\ & \Sigma(\log y)^2 & \Sigma(u + \alpha \log y)/y \\ & & \alpha\Sigma(\alpha - u)/y^2 \end{bmatrix} \begin{bmatrix} {}^{j+1}a - {}^j a \\ {}^{j+1}\alpha - {}^j\alpha \\ {}^{j+1}\theta - {}^j\theta \end{bmatrix} = \begin{bmatrix} \Sigma u \\ -\Sigma u \log y \\ -\alpha\Sigma u/y \end{bmatrix}$$

where $y = x + \theta$, and the Information Matrix is symmetric.

Using initial estimates of $\theta = 0$, and a and α obtained from ordinary least squares estimates of the basic Pareto function, iterations can then be continued until the adjustments are negligible. After the final iteration the estimate of σ^2 is obtained using

$$^{j+1}\sigma^2 = \Sigma u^2/T$$

which results conveniently, and not surprisingly, from rearrangement of the relevant scoring equation.

Table 3.1 Maximum likelihood estimates of $N = A/(x + \theta)^\alpha$

Sample	Constant (log A)	α	θ	OLS estimate of α	Pareto's α
1 Angleterre 1843	20.001 (0.524)	1.718 (0.059)	123.959 (46.244)	1.556 (0.039)	1.50
2 Angleterre 1879/80	19.123 (0.229)	1.355 (0.028)	−27.933 (14.535)	1.395 (0.020)	1.35
3 Villes Italiennes	22.300 (0.353)	1.566 (0.036)	346.36 (94.508)	1.434 (0.028)	1.45
4 Saxe 1880	23.576 (0.063)	1.632 (0.007)	84.45 (11.081)	1.589 (0.014)	1.58
5 Saxe 1886	22.854 (0.065)	1.515 (0.007)	0.543 (10.944)	1.514 (0.005)	1.51
6 Bale	17.789 (0.265)	1.226 (0.026)	−80.435 (77.757)	1.249 (0.017)	−
7 Oldenbourg 1890	27.918 (1.115)	2.376 (0.114)	1108.86 (210.969)	1.634 (0.100)	1.465
8 Crédit Foncier de France 1888	13.699 (0.127)	1.601 (0.023)	9.186 (0.611)	1.089 (0.087)	1.5773
9 Crédit Foncier de France 1895	14.445 (0.289)	1.894 (0.052)	6.773 (0.969)	1.359 (0.096)	1.8172
10 Austria 1891	31.756 (0.705)	2.972 (0.075)	388.75 (91.385)	2.697 (0.039)	2.7114
11 Wartemberg 1890	20.520 (0.218)	1.488 (0.023)	458.27 (41.971)	1.191 (0.058)	1.4186
12 Amburgo 1891	18.806 (0.182)	1.111 (0.018)	−102.005 (43.515)	1.146 (0.013)	1.1308
13 Schaumbourg Lippe 1893	16.632 (0.723)	1.299 (0.094)	9.472 (51.087)	1.282 (0.031)	1.2983
14 Zurich 1891	27.444 (0.907)	2.389 (0.101)	263.077 (93.940)	2.103 (0.049)	−
15 Wartemberg 1890	37.685 (1.521)	3.474 (0.160)	1539.08 (96.820)	2.030 (0.158)	2.881
16 Brema	17.444 (0.279)	1.124 (0.029)	−179.871 (55.794)	1.196 (0.025)	1.1814
17 Sassonia Weimia Eisenach 1892	23.386 (0.395)	1.860 (0.044)	348.59 (53.588)	1.563 (0.037)	1.6305 1.7342

Standard errors are given in parentheses.
Source: Samples 1 to 7 are distributions given in 'La Courbe de la Répartition de la Richesse' (1896), *Universite de Lausanne*, Recueil publié par la Faculté de Droit à l'occasion de l'exposition nationale Suisse, Geneva, 1896. Samples 8 to 17 are from 'Aggiunta allo studio della curve entrate', *Giornale degli Economisti*, January, 1897, pp. 15-26.

The above routine was applied to the data used by Pareto, and the results given in table 3.1. It can be seen that most of the values of θ are highly significant. They certainly do not justify Pareto's remarks about the relative values of θ. It is also instructive to compare the value for Oldenbourg with that given by Pareto. Furthermore only four of the values of θ are negative, again contradicting Pareto's remark that θ is negative for earnings from employment.

The above results clearly show that Pareto's statements concerning the general form of the upper tail of the income distribution are not supported by the evidence that he actually used. Furthermore some of his statements are, on closer examination, not consistent. It is also rather surprising that Pareto should publish only one estimate of his more general equation, when he claimed to have obtained many others. His summary, in terms of the sign of θ for different sources of income, is not confirmed by the data, but could easily have been checked by Pareto from the convexity or concavity of the double-log graphs. There is no explanation of how such estimates were obtained – though at that date any interactive method would have been extremely laborious. It seems that Pareto overstated his case somewhat.

Further Reading

This chapter is based on Creedy (1977b), and was influenced by the discussion of Pareto's views in Brown (1976). The method of estimation has been applied to recreational demand in Cheshire and Stabler (1976). A useful early discussion of Pareto's 'law' is Macaulay (1922). An interesting discussion of the estimation of the basic Pareto distribution is provided by Bowley (1926, pp. 346–8), and estimation using grouped data is treated in detail in Aigner and Goldberger (1970). Josiah Stamp used the Pareto distribution to concentrate the search for tax evaders in Britain, and much later the problem of estimation using under-reported data is examined by Hinckley and Revankar (1977). Stochastic models giving rise to the Pareto distribution are presented in Wold and Whittle (1957), Mandelbrot (1960), Steindl (1965), and Champernowne (1953), whose model was extended by Shorrocks (1976). A hierarchical model giving rise to a Pareto upper tail is given in the well known work by Lydall (1968), although a hierarchical model giving rise to the lognormal distribution is contained in the little known book by Tuck (1954).

Part III

Changes in Relative Earnings

4

Regression Analysis of Earnings Changes

This chapter presents a number of regression models for the analysis of changes in relative earnings among a group of individuals over time. Longitudinal data are still rare, and in most cases information about individuals' characteristics are quite limited. The methods described here are later applied to constant samples of individuals of the same age (or cohort). Information about each individual is usually too short for the estimation of models in which individuals are assumed to have different parameters. An important motivation for the present approach is that it is required to have a model that can be easily integrated into much wider models of economic behaviour, where earnings dynamics are relevant.

The starting point of the analysis is a simple decomposition of proportionate earnings changes from one period to the next. The period of analysis used is obviously important, and will be examined in section 4.3 below, but the present discussion is in terms of annual earnings. For any individual the proportionate change in income from one year to the next is regarded as being the same as that of the geometric mean income of the age group, apart from an additive stochastic term which governs the extent of movements within the distribution. This framework can therefore be written

$$\frac{1}{y_{it}} \frac{dy_{it}}{dt} = \frac{1}{m_t} \frac{dm_t}{dt} + u_{it} \qquad (4.1)$$

$$= f(t) + u_{it}$$

where y_{it} is individual i's income at age t, m_t is the geometric mean income in age group t and u_{it} is a stochastic component.

Thus, everyone's income is assumed to change by the same proportion, except for the term u_{it}, whose expected value must by definition be zero. The framework represented by equation (4.1), and which as yet has no empirical content, has obvious affinities with that of Friedman and Kuznets (1945) so $f(t)$ and u_{it} may (loosely) be referred to as 'permanent' and 'transitory' components respectively of the *change* in income. They should not, however, be confused with their use by Friedman (1957), where the term 'permanent' as applied to *levels* of income has a completely different and better known meaning. Friedman and Kuznets (1945) ascribed the relative income changes to 'chance' factors, although it should be noted that they examined distributions for all age groups combined, unlike the present context. The characteristics of u_{it} therefore determine the nature of changes in relative income status within the cohort. Section 4.1 presents three alternative specifications of u_{it}, and section 4.2 then shows the different implications for the dispersion of annual earnings. There is of course a fundamental link between earnings mobility and the extent to which measured dispersion is affected by taking longer 'accounting periods', and this issue will be examined in detail in Part V of this book. The estimation problems raised by the alternative specifications are then considered in section 4.3, and some empirical results are presented in section 4.4.

It is perhaps worth stressing again that it is *not* the purpose of this Part of the book to produce a stochastic model of the genesis of income distribution, in the tradition of the models mentioned in chapter 1. Indeed, Part V provides an explicit treatment of 'births' and 'deaths', and the effect of aggregating over age groups. The search for implied 'stable' distributions, after a possibly very long time interval, has no role in this context.

4.1   Alternative Specifications

In order to abstract, for the time being, from changes in the geometric mean income of the age group or cohort, it is convenient to consider proportionate changes in the ratio of income to geometric mean income. Then

$$\frac{m_t}{y_{it}} \frac{\mathrm{d}}{\mathrm{d}t} \left(\frac{y_{it}}{m_t} \right) = u_{it} \qquad (4.2)$$

and defining $x_{it} = \log y_{it}$, $\mu_t = \log m_t$ and $z_{it} = \log(y_{it}/m_t) = x_{it} - \mu_t$, equation (4.2) can be rewritten simply as

$$dz_{it}/dt = u_{it} \qquad (4.3)$$

Gibrat's 'Law of Proportionate Effect'

One of the earliest and perhaps best known stochastic models is that of Gibrat (1931), which he applied to all age groups combined. Gibrat's assumption can nevertheless be adopted for the present context, and gives the simplest mobility process. The process assumes that the u_{it} are distributed independently of previous changes, have constant variance, σ_u^2, and do not depend on the relative income position in the previous period. The Law of Proportionate Effect therefore implies a simple first order autoregressive form. It is most convenient to rewrite (4.3) in discrete form, using these assumptions, to give

$$z_{it} = z_{it-1} + u_{it} \qquad (4.4)$$

Galtonian Regression Towards the Mean

It was suggested by Kalecki (1946) that there may be a tendency for those in the higher deciles of the income distribution to obtain proportionately smaller increases than those in the lower deciles. This type of phenomenon is precisely Galton's (1889) concept of 'regression towards the mean', which he proposed in connection with the inheritance of genetic characteristics. In this context it is most conveniently specified by subtracting

$$(1 - \beta) \log(x_{it-1}/m_{t-1}) = (1 - \beta)z_{it-1}$$

from the right-hand side of (4.4.). Thus when earnings are below the geometric mean ($x_{it-1} < m_{t-1}$), the logarithm of relative earnings is negative, and the average change is greater than that of the geometric mean, so long as $\beta < 1$. This gives

$$z_{it} = \beta z_{it-1} + u_{it} \qquad (4.5)$$

and β is the 'regression' coefficient. It is in some ways unfortunate that Galton's term 'regression' has come to be used much more generally to describe a coefficient in a linear model. The Gibrat model is thus a special case of (4.5) where $\beta = 1$, and if $\beta < 1$ there is a systematic 'egalitarian' tendency for those in the higher income groups ($x_{it} > m_t$) to receive, *on average*, lower proportionate increases than those in the lower groups.

Some idea of the order of magnitude involved when considering Galtonian 'regression' may be obtained by considering the extent to which individuals in particular quantiles of the income distribution obtain, on average, different percentage changes. For example, for a value of β of 0.98, the average percentage increase for those with incomes of $\frac{1}{4}$ of the geometric mean is 2.8 percentage points higher than for those with incomes at the geometric mean. This is reduced to 1.4 for those with incomes of $\frac{1}{2}$ of the geometric mean. A small change in β to 0.95 increases the respective values to 7 and 3.5 percentage points, while for β as low as 0.75 the differences become as high as 41 and 19. The first example is obtained using the fact that $-(1 - \beta) \log(0.25) = 0.028$. The percentage change is then obtained as $\exp(0.028) - 1$. For a decrease in income the percentage reduction would be calculated as $1 - \exp(\text{log-change})$. Thus log-changes are symmetric about the geometric mean, although this is not the case for percentage changes.

The Galton model was first applied by Hart and Prais (1956) to the analysis of changes in the size of firms. They suggested that the correlation coefficient between z_t and z_{t-1}, denoted ρ, can be used as an inverse measure of size mobility. A further interesting result is then obtained, using the simple connection between the regression and correlation coefficients in a bivariate model. If σ_t^2 denotes the variance of x_t, then the well known result is obtained that, since $\beta = \text{cov}(z_t z_{t-1})/\sigma_{t-1}^2$ and $\rho = \text{cov}(z_t z_{t-1})/\sigma_t \sigma_{t-1}$,

$$\beta/\rho = \sigma_t/\sigma_{t-1} \tag{4.6}$$

The change in the variance of log-earnings from one year to the next can therefore be interpreted in terms of the relative sizes of the regression and correlation coefficients. This clearly shows that judgements about changes in 'inequality' cannot be made on the basis only of comparative static analyses. The value of σ^2 can increase even when egalitarian changes are taking place. Alternative situations are discussed in Hart (1976, pp. 112–14).

Serial Correlation

It may be thought that individuals in certain occupations are able to move through the income distribution of their contemporaries in a fairly systematic way; or indeed that significant improvements may depend crucially on previous success. This may apply, for example, in professions where 'merit' awards are commonly paid, or where prospects for increasing income depend on a reputation which is established on the basis of previous work. Where successive proportionate changes in income are correlated this means that the relative stability of an individual's position in the distribution is increased; income depends on that of the past few years rather than simply that of the previous year. This can be seen by assuming a first order autoregressive form for the u_{it}, such that

$$u_{it} = \gamma u_{it-1} + \epsilon_{it} \tag{4.7}$$

where γ is assumed to be the same for all individuals, and ϵ_{it} is now distributed independently of previous values with (constant) variance σ_ϵ^2, say. Combining this with equation (4.5), and eliminating the us from each, gives the reduced form

$$z_{it} = (\gamma + \beta)z_{it-1} - \gamma\beta z_{it-2} + \epsilon_{it} \tag{4.8}$$

which is a second order autoregressive process. It will be seen in the next section that, for annual earnings, the serial correlation coefficient is often negative, whereas for the growth of firms it is more often positive.

The total effect of a small amount of Galtonian regression with negative serial correlation can perhaps be seen more clearly from table 4.1. This shows, for values of β and γ of 0.96 and -0.3 respectively, the average percentage change in income that would be expected for various alternative 'previous changes' ϵ_{t-1} and 'current relative positions' x_t/m_t. This change is of course in addition to the systematic change in m_t for the group as a whole.

Table 4.1 Average percentage annual income change in addition to the increase in mean income; by relative position and previous relative change

ϵ_{t-1} \ x_t/m_t	0.25	0.50	2.0	4.0
-0.3	15.7	12.5	6.4	3.6
-0.2	12.2	9.2	3.3	0.5
$+0.2$	-0.5	-3.1	-8.4	-10.9
$+0.3$	-3.4	-6.0	-11.1	-13.5

$\beta = 0.96$; $\gamma = -0.3$.

For example, those who earn 25% of the geometric mean earnings and experienced a proportionate (relative) decrease of -0.3 in the previous period would, *on average*, experience a (relative) increase of 15.7%. Those who previously experienced a relative increase in earnings would, on average, experience a subsequent decrease, even if their current earnings are below the geometric mean.

4.2   Mobility and Earnings Dispersion Over Time

It has already been suggested that earnings mobility must be closely linked with the relationship between measured inequality and the time period over which earnings are measured. This will be examined in Part V, but it is first useful to derive the implications of the alternative specifications of mobility for changes in a static measure of dispersion over time. The most tractable measure of dispersion to use is obviously the variance of the logarithms of earnings, which is denoted σ_t^2 for age group t. Taking variances of (4.4) gives, since $z_{it} = x_{it} - \mu_t$,

$$\sigma_t^2 = \sigma_{t-1}^2 + \sigma_u^2$$

whence continual substitution gives

$$\sigma_t^2 = \sigma_0^2 + \sigma_u^2 t \tag{4.9}$$

with σ_0^2 defined as the variance of log-income in the year of entry into the occupation, or labour market. Thus Gibrat's process in this context implies that the variance of the logarithms of earnings grows linearly with age. This will be examined below, but Gibrat originally applied his law to all age groups combined, for which a continually increasing dispersion seems much less plausible. It was this feature that motivated Kalecki's (1945) suggestion of including regression towards the mean (although it will be shown in chapter 9 that a birth and death process can ensure stability of the aggregate distribution).

Continual substitution, from (4.5), gives

$$z_{it} = \beta^t z_{i0} + \sum_{j=1}^{t} \beta^{t-j} u_{ij} \tag{4.10}$$

Taking variances, using the sum of a geometric progression to evaluate the second term, then

$$\sigma_t^2 = \frac{\sigma_u^2}{1 - \beta^2} + \left(\sigma_0^2 + \frac{\sigma_u^2}{1 - \beta^2} \right) \beta^{2t} \tag{4.11}$$

For large t, and $\beta < 1$, the right-hand side of (4.11) tends to the constant value $\sigma_u^2/(1 - \beta^2)$. This kind of regression therefore tends to stabilize the degree of inequality within a particular cohort, while allowing mobility within the distribution.

Serial Correlation

Where serial correlation exists along with regression, the variance σ_t^2 is rather more cumbersome to derive. From (4.10) above, and dropping i subscripts

$$\sigma_t^2 = \beta^{2t}\sigma_0^2 + E\left(\sum_j \beta^{t-j}u_j\right)\left(\sum_j \beta^{t-j}u_j\right) \tag{4.12}$$

With no serial correlation the cross product terms in (4.12) cancel, although they must now be included to give

$$\sigma_t^2 = \beta^{2t}\sigma_0^2 + E\sum_j \beta^{2(t-j)}u_j^2 + E\sum_{i \neq j}\sum \beta^{(t-i)(t-j)}u_i u_j$$

and using the fact that

$$E(u_t^2) = \sigma_\epsilon^2 \sum_{t=1}^{t} \gamma^{2i}$$

and $E(u_t u_{t-s}) = \gamma^s E(u_t^2)$ this can be written as

$$\sigma_t^2 = \beta^{2t}\sigma_0^2 + \sigma_\epsilon^2 \sum_{j=1}^{t}\sum_{i=1}^{j}\rho^{2(t-j)}\gamma^{2i} +$$

$$+ 2\sigma_\epsilon^2 \sum_{j=1}^{t-1}\sum_{i=j+1}^{t}\sum_{r=0}^{i}\beta^{(t-i)(t-j)}\gamma^{2r+i-j} \tag{4.13}$$

which is clearly inconvenient. The case of no regression combined with serial correlation can be found simply by setting $\beta = 1$. But even in this case in practice it will not be possible to discriminate between the more complex kind of earnings changes and the simple Gibrat model, given only a series of σ_t^2s. This is because the relation between the latter and t is only non-linear for low values of t and rapidly becomes linear. Static measures of dispersion for a variety of age groups do not therefore provide sufficient information to allow clear inferences to be made about the mobility process. Longitudinal data are required, although the estimation problems are not quite straightforward, as shown in the next section.

4.3 Some Estimation Problems

Before examining the estimation of the regression model it is worth recalling the usually limited nature of the data that are available (other than perhaps the extensive longitudinal surveys carried out over many years in the United States). A typical situation is that individual observations on a particular cohort are available, covering a small number of time periods, and it is assumed that the parameters of the model are the same for all individuals. Thus it is important to stress that regression models of mobility do not correspond to conventional time series analyses. All the relevant summations are over individuals, not time. For example, in a time series context it is well known that the estimation of a first order autoregressive equation such as (4.5) gives biased estimates if the disturbances are serially correlated. Furthermore the use of the observed deviations, from an ordinary least squares (OLS) regression, in estimating the serial correlation coefficient also leads to bias. Malinvaud (1970, p. 556) demonstrates that the sum of the OLS estimates described above nevertheless provides a consistent estimate of the sum of the parameters β and γ. These results cannot be *directly* applied in the present context although a similar set of results can be obtained, as shown below.

A further problem arises over the choice of the most appropriate time period of analysis; whether earnings should be measured over consecutive weeks, months or years. Individuals may change jobs or suffer spells of sickness and/or unemployment within a year, and of course earnings changes will not take place conveniently at the beginning of some arbitrarily chosen period. However, the period chosen will have implications for the interpretation of results, as also shown below. In some cases observations may not cover *consecutive* time periods, and there may be uneven intervals between periods.

Estimation of the Second Order Model

The second order autoregressive equation (4.8) was shown to arise from the combination of Galtonian regression towards the mean with serial correlation in the stochastic term u_{it}. Given observations on (at least) three consecutive periods, the most appropriate strategy is to start by estimating (4.8) using ordinary least squares. Rewrite (4.8) as

$$z_{it} = az_{it-1} + bz_{it-1} + \epsilon_{it} \qquad (4.14)$$

where $a = \gamma + \beta$ and $b = -\gamma\beta$. In practice the regression would be run using x_{it}, x_{it-1} and x_{it-2} as variables, and a constant term would then be included.

An immediate problem arises because of the fact that (4.14) does not contain an exogenous variable, so γ and β cannot be identified. There are two equations in the two 'unknowns' γ and β. However, using $\gamma = -b/\beta$ from (4.14) it can be seen that $\beta - b/\beta = a$, so

$$\beta^2 - a\beta - b = 0 \qquad (4.15)$$

Precisely the same equation is obtained for γ, so although there are two roots to the quadratic, a further assumption needs to be made in order to identify the parameters. In this context it seems quite reasonable to suppose that β will be close to unity, the largest root $\{\hat{a} + (\hat{a}^2 + 4\hat{b})^{1/2}\}/2$ is taken as the estimate of β (where $\hat{a}$ and $\hat{b}$ are the OLS estimates of a and b), and the smallest root is used as the estimate of γ. The same suggestion has also been made by Chesher (1973, 1979, p. 407). Having obtained the parameter estimates, it then remains to calculate their sampling variances. This is easily achieved following the method given by Goldberger (1964, p. 124); thus, for example,

$$V(\hat{\beta}) = V(\hat{a})(d\hat{\beta}/d\hat{a})^2 + V(\hat{b})(d\hat{\beta}/d\hat{a})$$
$$+ 2 \operatorname{cov}(\hat{a}, \hat{b})(d\hat{\beta}/d\hat{a})(d\hat{\beta}/d\hat{b}) \qquad (4.16)$$

It should be noted that this method requires the assumption, implicit in the above discussion, that β remains constant over the period of observation. This procedure is more awkward if consecutive observations are not available. Suppose, for example, that first order serial correlation applies, and that data are recorded at two-year intervals. Then it can be shown that

$$z_{it} = (\gamma^3 + \beta^2)z_{it-2} - \gamma^3\beta^2 z_{it-4} + \eta_{it} \qquad (4.17)$$

where η_{it} satisfies the conditions required for the application of OLS. The serial correlation cannot so easily be avoided if the observations are not separated by an even number of years, however.

Some idea of the effect of using different time periods can be seen by taking the simple case of a comparison between weekly and fortnightly earnings. If weekly earnings follow the first order Galton process, then

$$z = \beta z_{-1} + u \tag{4.18}$$

where the i and t subscripts have been omitted for convenience. Then the relationship between variables measured over two weeks would be

$$(z + z_{-1}) = \beta^2(z_{-2} + z_{-3}) + \{u + (1 + \beta)u_{-1} + \beta u_{-2}\} \tag{4.19}$$

Similarly the disturbance term in the relationship between $z_{-2} + z_{-3}$ and $z_{-4} + z_{-5}$ is given by $u_{-2} + (1 - \beta)u_{-3} + \beta u_{-4}$. Denote these disturbances v and v_{-1}. If there is a first order autoregressive process in the us, such that

$$u = \gamma u_{-1} + \epsilon \tag{4.20}$$

then of course $V(u) = \sigma_\epsilon^2/(1 - \gamma^2)$ and $E(\epsilon \epsilon_{-s}) = \gamma^s \sigma_\epsilon^2$. Using these results it can be shown that the covariance between v and v_{-1} is given by

$$E(vv_{-1}) = \sigma_\epsilon^2\{\gamma^2(1 + \beta^2) + \beta(1 + \gamma^4) + (1 + \beta)^2(\gamma + \gamma^2 + \gamma^3)\} \tag{4.21}$$

Now suppose that $\gamma = -0.4$ and $\beta = 0.8$. Substitution into (4.21) shows that the term in curly brackets is equal to 0.098, so although week-to-week earnings are negatively correlated, there is slight positive serial correlation in the relation between successive fortnightly earnings.

The Galton Model

It may perhaps be thought that, if cross sectional rather than time series data are used to estimate the basic Galton model of (4.5), the well known results concerning bias, in the presence of serial correlation, would not apply. This approach was taken in, for example, Thatcher (1971). However, it is not difficult to show (following the same procedure as in Malinvaud, but allowing for the fact that all summations are over cross sections) that the OLS estimator is biased and inconsistent. An alternative proof has also been given in Chesher (1979, pp. 405-6). The probability limit of the OLS estimator for β is in fact $(\beta + \gamma)/(1 + \gamma\beta)$, which is precisely the same as in the time series context. If the OLS residuals from several bivariate regressions (that is, z on z_{-1} and z_{-1} on z_{-2}) are used to estimate γ, this also gives inconsistent results although the sum of the separate estimates of γ and β is a consistent estimator for their sum. If there is negative serial correlation, the more usual case for earnings (although not for firms), then the OLS estimate is biased downwards.

The Galton model has also been estimated using bivariate regressions, but relating earnings in one week to earnings in the corresponding week of the previous year, as in the *Department of Employment Gazette* (April, 1973; see also January 1977). However it is not appropriate to interpret the regression coefficient as an estimate of the value of β as if it were relevant to annual earnings. This statement is true *even if* there is no serial correlation (either week-to-week or year-to-year), except in the simple case where earnings are the same in every week of the relevant year. In the usual case the estimate will be biased downwards by an amount that depends on the variation of weekly earnings within the year.

Having compared alternative specifications and estimation methods, the following section applies the model to data for the UK and Sweden.

4.4 Some Empirical Results

The paucity of suitable data for the analysis of earnings mobility has already been mentioned. In Britain, until the early 1970s only the studies of Vandome (1958) and Prest and Stark (1967) used information about the earnings of individuals in more than one year. These data, from the Oxford surveys of the 1950s, and the 105th Inland Revenue *Report*, covered only two years and cannot therefore be used for the study of mobility processes described above. Following the suggestion of Hart (1968), Thatcher (1971) examined data provided by the DHSS, for 1963 and 1964, but the data tapes were then destroyed following a change of computing system. The weekly earnings in two years, from the *New Earnings Survey* and used in the *Gazette* (April, 1973), have already been mentioned in section 4.3. The first substantial samples of British data were drawn by the DHSS specifically for the studies by Hart (1976, 1976a), although these did not cover consecutive years. The collection of longitudinal data has proceeded very slowly in most other countries, and the most extensive data are now available for the United States.

The purpose of this section is to compare relative income changes of individuals in Britain and Sweden over the three years

1971, 1972 and 1973. The British data were provided by the Department of Health and Social Security for three cohorts of males born in 1923, 1933 and 1943; while the Swedish data are for cohorts born in 1913, 1918, 1923, 1928 and 1933, and were provided by the National Central Bureau of Statistics. For the British data annual earnings are from all sources as defined for income tax purposes, while Swedish data are of 'total net income' (the sum of earnings and income from all sources, less certain expenses such as interest payments).

In making comparisons between two countries it is of course always important to consider the possible differences that may arise simply because the data do not refer to exactly the same concept of income, or because the method of sampling is not the same in each country. One feature common to the data of both countries is the exclusion from the samples of individuals who had no income in any of the relevant years. Those who leave and subsequently re-enter the labour force within the period (and, in the case of the Swedish cohorts, have no other source of income) are therefore excluded. In both countries income is measured over a period of 12 months (either the tax year for Great Britain, or the calendar year for Sweden), but of course this may not necessarily be the appropriate accounting period to use. Individuals may experience variations in income within a year; some are paid hourly and have the opportunity to work overtime, some experience sickness or unemployment at some time within the period (which may affect earning ability) and some may change jobs, possibly in order to improve their prospects. Clearly not all individuals receive regular annual income increases at the beginning of each financial year. However, in the absence of more detailed data, there is no real alternative to measuring income for the whole year.

The analysis proceeds as described in section 4.3, involving first the estimation of a second order autoregressive equation. Regression results for the three years 1971-2-3 are given in table 4.2 for the five Swedish cohorts. The corresponding estimates of β and γ are presented in table 4.3. Table 4.3 shows very little variation between cohorts in the value of $\hat{\beta}$, which is about 0.95. The results also indicate that there is a certain amount of negative serial correlation in year-to-year relative changes, with values of $\hat{\gamma}$ of about −0.3 (again the differences between cohorts are not significant). This indicates, for example, that each additional relative increase in income of ten per cent in one period would, on average,

Table 4.2 Regressions of the logarithms of earnings 1971-2-3: Swedish cohorts (dependent variable = z_{73})

Cohort	Independent variables		R^2	N
	z_{72}	z_{71}		
1913	0.716	0.218	0.724	905
	(0.039)	(0.038)		
1918	0.602	0.325	0.748	982
	(0.028)	(0.031)		
1923	0.560	0.334	0.696	1112
	(0.031)	(0.032)		
1928	0.669	0.253	0.768	1120
	(0.032)	(0.032)		
1933	0.663	0.188	0.688	954
	(0.034)	(0.034)		

Standard errors are given in parentheses.

Table 4.3 Estimates of β and γ: Swedish cohorts

Cohort	$\hat{\beta}$	$\hat{\gamma}$
1913	0.946	−0.230
	(0.016)	(0.039)
1918	0.946	−0.344
	(0.014)	(0.030)
1923	0.922	−0.362
	(0.014)	(0.033)
1928	0.939	−0.270
	(0.012)	(0.033)
1933	0.877	−0.214
	(0.017)	(0.037)

Standard errors are given in parentheses.

be followed by a further relative decrease of three per cent in the next period.

For comparison, regressions for three different samples of each of the three British cohorts are shown in table 4.4, with the corresponding estimates of β and γ in table 4.5. The sample denoted

Table 4.4 Regression of the logarithms of earnings 1971-2-3: British cohorts (dependent variable $= z_{73}$)

Cohort and sample		Independent variables			
		z_{72}	z_{71}	R^2	N
1923	ALL	0.498	0.363	0.775	865
		(0.030)	(0.031)		
	AFE	0.516	0.382	0.878	654
		(0.035)	(0.036)		
	FE	0.806	0.119	0.919	360
		(0.060)	(0.061)		
1933	ALL	0.635	0.219	0.715	744
		(0.044)	(0.045)		
	AFE	0.750	0.134	0.829	610
		(0.053)	(0.055)		
	FE	0.733	0.150	0.819	377
		(0.075)	(0.080)		
1943	ALL	0.640	0.219	0.490	841
		(0.051)	(0.053)		
	AFE	0.802	0.110	0.708	670
		(0.051)	(0.053)		
	FE	0.794	0.147	0.743	358
		(0.084)	(0.087)		

Values for the samples of fully and almost fully employed (AFE) are taken from Creedy and Hart (1979, table 3).

Table 4.5 Estimates of β and γ: British cohorts

Cohort and sample		$\hat{\beta}$	$\hat{\gamma}$
1923	ALL	0.901	−0.403
	AFE	0.927	−0.412
	FE	0.933	−0.128
1933	ALL	0.883	−0.248
	AFE	0.899	−0.149
	FE	0.900	−0.167
1943	ALL	0.887	−0.247
	AFE	0.922	−0.119
	FE	0.950	−0.155

'ALL' consists of all individuals with a complete record of earnings, National Insurance contributions and credits in all years, irrespective of the number of weeks worked in each year. The sample denoted 'AFE' consists of a subsample of those in 'ALL' who had paid at least 48 National Insurance contributions in every year. Finally, the sample 'FE' is a further subsample consisting of only those who were fully employed over the three consecutive years (that is, paid 52 contributions). Although there is consistently less 'regression' as the proportion of fully employed within the sample increases, there is not such a systematic change in $\hat{\gamma}$.

The results for Britain and Sweden show surprisingly little difference, as can be seen by a comparison of tables 4.2 and 4.4. It may, however, be suggested that the specification of mobility used here does not measure all aspects of mobility. For instance, the British estimates refer only to full-time workers. Differences in labour force participation between Britain and Sweden and occupational differences may give differences in mobility between the two countries which might be revealed by a more detailed model and further data. Further disaggregation of the Swedish data into broad occupational groups does in fact reveal differences, particularly in the estimates of γ, between occupations and cohorts.

The information about British occupations is extremely limited, but data covering the same three years were provided by a special survey of professional chemists, who were members of the Royal Institute of Chemistry (now the Royal Society of Chemistry). The survey was of a random sample of members who were all aged 47 years in October 1973. Respondents were asked to give their annual earnings from 1971 onwards, with all the usual precautions having been made to ensure anonymity. When equation (4.14) was fitted to these data (246 individuals) the following results were obtained:

$$z_t = 1.0358z_{t-1} - 0.0594z_{t-2} \quad R^2 = 0.947$$
$$(0.0010) \quad (0.009)$$

where t is January 1973, so annual income is from January 1972 until January 1973. This implies values of 0.975 and 0.061 for $\hat{\beta}$ and $\hat{\gamma}$ respectively, which indicate very little 'regression' and serial correlation. It is quite possible that the observed *aggregate* 'regression' and serial correlation could result from the heterogeneity of the samples, with more homogeneous groups following the Gibrat process more closely.

Further Reading

This chapter is based largely on Creedy (1974). The results for chemists are taken from Creedy (1975a), and problems arising from using different time periods are from Creedy (1975b). The results for various cohorts are from Creedy and Hart (1979) for the UK, and Creedy *et al.* (1981) for Sweden. Various problems of estimation are also examined by Hart (1974), who examined earnings mobility further in Hart (1976, 1976a). A more recent general discussion of earnings mobility, inequality and regression is by Hart (1983). Multiple-component models of earnings mobility, where much more detailed and extensive data are available, are examined in, for example, Jöreskog (1978). The methods have been used by Lillard and Weiss (1979), and Lillard and Willis (1978), using US data. Useful introductions to the techniques and literature of these methods are contained in Long (1983, 1983a).

5

Matrix Analysis of Mobility

In examining almost any aspect of mobility in social systems, the use of discrete time, discrete state models has been very popular. Many examples can be found in areas such as labour mobility between occupations, firms and regions; the movement among labour market states of employment, sickness and unemployment; mobility among social classes of different generations of families; and progression through the various states of the education and health care systems. Many empirical studies of earnings mobility have also presented estimated transition matrices, covering movements among income groups or quantiles between two particular dates. Such matrices have been used for a number of purposes. In some cases they are used simply as a descriptive device; in others they are used to calculate alternative measures of mobility (obtained as functions of the elements of the matrix); and sometimes the implied equilibrium distributions are obtained. There is of course some overlap between the last two uses, especially where proposed mobility measures depend on the rate at which convergence to equilibrium is attained. The descriptive role of basic mobility matrices is also enhanced by the calculation of measures such as the implied average length of time spent in each state.

Despite its popularity, very little use will be made of the transition matrix framework in the present book. Instead, section 5.1 provides a 'decomposition' of the usual transition matrix in order to examine the assumptions underlying Gibrat's Law of Proportionate Effect. Section 5.2 then explores the use of the transition matrix approach to earnings mobility using continuous time models.

The preference in favour of the regression models presented in the previous chapter may be justified for several reasons. The basic analysis of earnings mobility does not deal with dichotomous variables, and so it is necessary to specify a set of earnings groups. The choice of grouping method is far from being an arbitrary decision. When there is general growth in earnings over the period then some method of adjustment must be used in order to focus on relative changes, but this is unnecessary in the logarithmic regression framework. The latter framework also uses a much smaller number of parameters, and more easily allows the basic features of earnings mobility to be integrated into life cycle earnings models, and into wider economic models (as demonstrated in later Parts of this book). Aggregation is also more easily carried out using the regression framework (chapter 7 and Part V below). Furthermore, the statistical properties of regression models are well established, while the sampling properties of many aspects of transition matrices have yet to be fully explored (especially the mobility measures, characteristic roots and the continuous time models which present additional special difficulties).

The Regression Model and Transition Matrices

It may first be noted briefly that if a transition matrix is required the results of chapter 4 can be used to generate the implied transition proportions for movement among specified earnings groups over time. This can easily be done once the joint distribution of earnings in two years has been specified. For example, in many later chapters it will be assumed that earnings in each year can be approximated by the lognormal distribution (remembering that it is *not* the purpose of the analysis to provide a model of the genesis of any functional form). Hence earnings in years t and s follow the bivariate lognormal, and log-earnings follow the bivariate Normal distribution. From the standard properties of the latter, it can be seen that the conditional distribution of earnings in s, given earnings in t, is

$$\Lambda(y_s \,|\, \mu_s + \rho(\sigma_s/\sigma_t)\,(\log y_t - \mu_t),\, (1-\rho^2)\sigma_s^2) \qquad (5.1)$$

where ρ is the correlation between log-earnings in the two years, and μ_t and σ_t^2 are respectively the mean and variance of log-earnings in year t. The term $\rho\sigma_s/\sigma_t$ is of course the regression coefficient, β, whose value clearly depends on the assumptions made concerning relative earnings mobility. For the simple Gibrat process it is unity, and for the Galtonian 'regression' it is β^{s-t}. Then for periods t and $t + \tau$, the conditional distribution is

$$\Lambda(y_{t+\tau} \,|\, \mu_{t+\tau} + \beta^\tau(\log y_t - \mu_t),\, (\sigma_{t+\tau}^2 - \sigma_t^2)\beta^{2\tau}) \qquad (5.2)$$

This enables a matrix of age-specific transition probabilities for movement from one income class to another between any two years to be constructed by integrating (5.2) over the appropriate income range. The case of serially correlated changes is however more complicated, and is not treated here.

5.1 Testing Mobility Assumptions

A well known simple test of the assumption that individuals have the same transition probabilities irrespective of their past transitions among earnings groups (that the process is a first order Markov process) involves a comparison of the product of transition matrices for sub-periods with the observed matrix covering the whole period. This test was reported by Shorrocks (1976, p. 569), who used data relating to males born in 1933, for the years 1963, 1966 and 1970. (These data were compiled by the DHSS for Hart, 1973.) Where M_1 denotes the transition matrix for moves between 1963 and 1966, M_2 for moves between 1966 and 1970, and M_3 for observed moves over the whole period between 1963 and 1970, Shorrocks' showed that the diagonals of $M_1 M_2$ were consistently below those of M_3. This indicates that the number of 'stayers' in each earnings group is underestimated when using the sub-period matrices. This type of result has been reported by many researchers, especially in the context of occupational mobility. It is consistent with population heterogeneity, where the Markov assumption is appropriate to subgroups in the population, or with the rejection of the Markov process even for homogeneous populations. The first type of argument has led to the development of variants of the 'mover–stayer' model, and to the use of continuous time models with heterogeneous rates of change (discussed in the next section). Shorrocks (1976) retained the assumptions of population homogeneity and 'Proportionate Effect' (that the transition rates are independent of the current group occupied), and showed that the introduction of a second order process provided a statistically significant improvement over the simple model.

It is argued here however that an attempt should be made to isolate the effects of serial correlation and Galtonian regression in the transition matrix framework, just as in the previous chapter. This section therefore uses a more detailed decomposition than that used by Shorrocks, and also adds two more cohorts, using the data described and used in Hart (1976, Appendix A, p. 562). The data are for three cohorts born in 1923, 1933 and 1943, and for the youngest and oldest cohorts the data cover the years 1963, 1968 and 1973. All members of the samples paid at least 48 National Insurance contributions in each relevant year.

The procedure is described as follows. Movements between income groups (of equal logarithmic width, the same as in Hart, 1976, table 1, p. 553) are recorded over the three years in a table which presents both the changes made over the two relevant periods and the income class occupied in the middle year. An example is given in table 5.1 for the cohort born in 1933. The right-hand column total shows the number moving between specified income groups between the first two years, while the body of the table shows the subsequent moves from the second to the third year. For example, of the 82 people who moved from class 5 to class 6 between 1963 and 1966, 36 individuals were also in class 6 in 1970, and 38 had returned to class 5 by 1970. It is important to note that the 'time unit' appropriate to the following analysis is regarded simply as the number of intervening years between observations. The fact that people may have made unobserved movements among various other income classes in intervening years is ignored.

Tables such as that shown in table 5.1 can then be used to separate the two effects that are produced when the process follows neither a first order Markov process nor the Law of Proportionate Effect. For example, for all those in any given income group in the second year a comparison of the number of class changes made between the first two years with the number made between the second two years can be made. A standard χ^2 test of independence of successive class changes can then be carried out for each income class for which sufficient observations are available. Similarly a comparison can be made *between* income classes, for all those in a cohort who experienced the same number of previous class changes.

Independence of Successive Class Changes

It is useful to introduce the notation used by Shorrocks (1976, p. 570), where P_{ijk} is the probability of a transition from class j to class k in the period from t to $t + 1$, given that class i was occupied at time $t - 1$. (Remember that here $t - 1$ means 1963, t means 1968 for cohorts born in 1923 and 1943, and so on.) The independence of successive class changes can then be tested by

Table 5.1   Earnings in 1963-66-70

		Income class in 1970															
'63	'66	1	2	3	4	5	6	7	8	9	10	11	12	13	14	15	
3 { 3	3	2	1														3
3	4		2	1													3
4 { 4	4	1	2	1	1												5
5	4	1	1														2
4	5				8	6		2									16
5 { 5	5	1	1		6	2											10
6	5				1	2											3
4	6				1	10	8	2									21
5	6				2	38	36	4	2								82
6 { 6	6					11	14	8									33
7	6						3	2		1							6
4	7					2	3										5
5	7				1	6	24	20	11		1						63
7 { 6	7					12	57	50	17								136
7	7					2	15	22	3								42
8	7					2											2
5	8					2	3	4	5	1							15
6	8						6	25	30	4							65
8 { 7	8					1	10	47	37	15	1						111
8	8						2	8	9	4	1						24
9	8							1	1								2
6	9						1	2	1	1							5
9 { 7	9		1					5	21	14	1						42
8	9							3	19	17	3						42
9	9							1	1		2						4
7	10									1	1						2
10 { 8	10									1	5	10					16
9	10									1	5	3					9
11 { 9	11						1				1	3					5

examining, *for each j*, the individuals making $k - j$ class changes between the second two years after making $j - i$ moves between the first two years. In this way any possible effect on $k - j$ of the class, j, occupied before the change can be isolated. This contrasts with the comparisons of $k - j$ against $j - i$ shown in Shorrocks (1976, p. 574), which are made over *all* income groups j. Using data from table 5.1, and for income class number 7 in 1966, the frequencies of successive changes are shown in table 5.2, where

54 Changes in relative earnings

some of the classes have been consolidated for the application of the χ^2 test. A standard χ^2 test of independence with four degrees of freedom can then be carried out. The results of repeating this exercise for each class j, and for each cohort, are given in table 5.3.

From table 5.3 it can be seen that the assumption of independence fails at the $2\frac{1}{2}$ per cent level only for the cohort born in 1923 and for those in income group 7 in 1968. It is interesting to compare this with a corresponding value of χ^2 using the table in Shorrocks (1976, p. 574) which shows class changes (using the

Table 5.2 Successive changes of cohort born in 1933, and in earnings class 7 in 1966

Class changes 1963-66 $(j-i)$	Class changes 1966-70 $(k-j)$			
	-2 and -1	0	1	Total
0	17	22	3	42
$+1$	69	50	17	136
2 and 3	31	20	12	63

Table 5.3 Changes between income classes (equal logarithmic width) for those in the same class before the change

Group	Class occupied	χ^2	Degrees of freedom
Cohort 1943	5	0.08	2
	6	8.44	4
	7	11.43	6
	8	5.31	6
Cohort 1933	5	2.34	2
	6	7.45	4
	7	6.51	4
	8	9.04	4
	9	1.23	1
Cohort 1923	6	1.78	2
	7	12.40	4
	8	0.18	1

Null hypothesis: Independence between successive changes.

same class widths as here; that is 0.1 in the logarithms of earnings taken to base 10) between 1963 and 6, and 1966 and 70, for cohort 1933. When this table is suitably consolidated the value of χ^2 with nine degrees of freedom is found to be 45.52. Thus the test unambiguously rejects the assumption of independence between successive class changes (the critical value of χ^2 at the $2\frac{1}{2}$ per cent level is 19.02) when all classes are aggregated – but rarely does so when the sample is further disaggregated according to the class occupied in the middle year. (The contrast is, however, slightly exaggerated since χ^2 is known to increase as the total number of observations increases, with no commensurate increase in the number of degrees of freedom.)

Independence of Income Class Occupied Before Change

Proceeding along similar lines, the assumption of 'Proportionate Effect' can be tested, independently of any possible effect that may be due to correlation between successive changes. This is carried out by collecting all individuals in each cohort who have experienced the same number of class changes between the first two years. A contingency table can then be constructed, for each value of $(j - i)$, showing the number of subsequent class changes $(k - j)$ according to the class, j, occupied in the middle year. An example is given in table 5.4 for the cohort born in 1933, and where $(j - i) = 1$; that is, those who moved up one class between 1963 and 1966. Again, a standard χ^2 test with nine degrees of freedom can be performed to test the maintained hypothesis of independence between the class occupied and the subsequent number of class changes. The results of repeating this, for all cases where sufficient observations are available, are given in table

Table 5.4   Changes between 1966 and 1970 for cohort 1933 for whom $j - i = 1$, by income class in 1966

Class in 1966 (j)	Class change 1966-70 ($k - j$)				
	-2	-1	0	1 or more	Total
5 and 6	2	46	42	8	98
7	12	57	50	17	136
8	11	47	37	16	111
9	3	19	17	3	42

Table 5.5   Changes between income classes (equal logarithmic width) for those with some previous change

Group	Number of class changes $(j - i)$	χ^2	Degrees of freedom
Cohort	1	7.91	2
1943	2	21.97	4
	3	33.04	6
	4	16.42	6
	5	0.31	1
Cohort	0	5.23	4
1933	1	9.61	9
	2	3.22	3
Cohort	0	5.17	2
1923	1	34.56	6
	2	11.48	6

Null hypothesis: independence between number of changes $(k - j)$ and class, j, occupied.

5.5. The assumption of independence between the class occupied and the subsequent number of class changes is rejected (at the $2\frac{1}{2}$ per cent level) for all values of $j - i$ in cohort 20 (except $j - i = 5$), and for cohort 40 when $j - i = 1$.

The main result of the above analysis is therefore that when mobility between earnings classes (of equal logarithmic width) is decomposed to isolate the possible separate effects of both the violation of the assumption of Proportionate Effect and that of a first order Markov process, then the performance of each of these assumptions is much improved. When only one of these assumptions is tested (assuming that the other one holds) it is found to be clearly rejected, but when the process is disaggregated to examine both assumptions simultaneously then their performance is seen to be relatively better.

5.2   Continuous Time Models

An alternative approach to the finding that a larger proportion of individuals remain in the same state for longer periods than predicted using a simple Markov transition matrix has been to allow for population heterogeneity. Two aspects of heterogeneity may be distinguished here. First, individuals may differ in their *rates* of movement through states, and secondly they may differ in the *types* of transition made at the time a move is actually made. This distinction can be most easily handled in the context of continuous time models, rather than the discrete time models in which movement is only 'allowed' at particular intervals. With a long time interval between observations the discrete time transition matrix approach cannot allow for unobserved multiple moves among states between the two observation points.

For the continuous time model, define the (i, j)th element of the matrix $P(t)$ as the proportion moving from state i to state j, from time 0 to time t. The transition matrix $P(t)$ is regarded as the solution to the set of differential equations

$$\mathrm{d}P(t)/\mathrm{d}t = QP(t) \tag{5.3}$$

If the initial condition $P(0) = I$ is imposed, then the solution to (5.3) is

$$P(t) = \exp(Qt) \tag{5.4}$$

The matrix Q is called the 'intensity matrix' and is the fundamental matrix of the continuous time model. Q has the following properties:

$$q_{ii} < 0 \qquad q_{ij} > 0 \qquad \sum_j q_{ij} = 0 \qquad \text{for all } i \tag{5.5}$$

where $q_{ij}/(-q_{ii})$ is the probability that an individual in state i will move to state j, given that a move is made, and $1/(-q_{ii})$ is the expected length of stay in state i.

These models have been investigated at length by Singer and Spilerman (1974, 1976), who have indicated how the distinction between the two types of heterogeneity, mentioned earlier, may be used to generate results concerning aggregation. They use a convenient factorization of the intensity matrix such that

$$Q = \Lambda(M - I) \tag{5.6}$$

where Λ is a diagonal matrix whose elements are $-q_{ii}$, $\{m_{ij}\} = \{-q_{ij}/q_{ii}\}$, $i \neq j$; and $m_{ii} = 0$. The matrix Λ contains the rates of movement out of states, and M governs the transitions followed when moves are actually made. In addition, if M is assumed to be the same for all individuals, if $\Lambda = \lambda I$ (the rates of movement are the same for all states) and if λ has a Gamma distribution over individuals, such that the density function is $g(\lambda) = \beta^\alpha \lambda^{\alpha-1} e^{-\beta\lambda} / \Gamma(\alpha)$, then the aggregate $P(t)$ matrix can be shown to be

$$P(t) = \{\beta/(\beta + t)\}^\alpha [I - \{t/(\beta + t)\} M]^{-\alpha} \tag{5.7}$$

In the context of earnings changes these assumptions seem to be rather restrictive. However, it seems useful to examine whether observed transition matrices, obtained from fairly aggregative data, can be regarded as being generated by the continuous time process described in (5.4). This requires the solution to (5.4), which is

$$Q = (1/t) \log P(t) \tag{5.8}$$

and which requires the calculation of the logarithm of a matrix. This raises severe difficulties since the logarithm may not exist, it may not be unique, and even if it is unique, the elements may not satisfy the conditions specified in (5.5). A unique solution exists when the characteristic roots of $P(t)$ are real and strictly positive, and if they are also distinct it is possible to use Sylvester's formula for a general function f of a matrix argument. For the square matrix A with distinct roots h_i

$$f(A) = \sum_i f(h_i) \sum_{j \neq i} \{(A - h_i I)/(h_i - h_j)\} \tag{5.9}$$

In practice a considerable number of transition matrices relating to earnings mobility are found to have positive, real and distinct roots, so a unique logarithm can be found using (5.9). However, very rarely are the conditions (5.5) satisfied, the usual problem being that some of the off-diagonals of Q are negative (although the other conditions are usually met). This is true of matrices for particular occupations, as well as for wider aggregates. The continuous time framework, while rather appealing in many ways, does not therefore offer very much scope in the present context, although it has been found helpful in other applications.

Further Reading

This chapter is based on Creedy (1978). An early influential analysis of social mobility using matrix methods is by Prais (1955). On the growth of firms there is Adelman (1958), and see also Hart (1962). For an earlier discussion of equilibrium income distributions see Vandome (1958). Shorrocks (1978) examines the measurement of mobility using matrices, and prefers the half life as a good compromise. A useful extended analysis of mobility is by Boudon (1973). Further Markov models of earnings mobility include McCall (1971), and the mover–stayer model was presented in Goodman (1961). A matrix framework for analysing social mobility, allowing for dependence on the past, is given by Stone (1973), whose method has been examined in the context of hierarchical models by Creedy (1977c). An application of continuous time models to labour market flows is given in Creedy and Disney (1981), and a Markov model of labour flows which explicitly allows for population heterogeneity is presented in Creedy and Disney (1981a). A useful text on stochastic models is Bartholomew (1973).

Part IV

The Age-Earnings Profile

6

The Changing Distribution of Earnings with Age

At the beginning of chapter 4 each individual's proportionate earnings change from one period to the next was decomposed into a systematic component depending on age, and a transitory component which affects *relative* earnings changes. Part III then concentrated on *relative* earnings mobility. The purpose of this Part is to examine the systematic component of each age group's earnings changes, and to combine this with the earlier results in order to produce a description of the changing distribution of earnings with age. Important requirements of any model are that it must have the advantages of describing a wide range of experience (different occupation groups, and wider aggregates, in many countries); of containing few, easily interpreted parameters; and of being very tractable when included in wider analyses of economic behaviour and income distribution.

The decomposition of equation (4.1) in fact follows the suggestion by Aitchison and Brown (1957, p. 109) that 'the earnings of an individual person through life may well be described by a stochastic process of the form $y_t = y_{t-1} \exp\{f(t) + u_t\}$, where the function $f(t)$ is chosen to describe the path of the median income through life and u_t is $N(0, \sigma_u^2)$ and independent of t'. The notation in this quotation has been changed slightly to conform with that of the present study. The assumption of lognormality for each age group implies that the median is equal to the geometric mean. Their statement about the properties of u_t was based on the observation, using cross sectional data for professions in Britain and in the United States, that the profile of σ_t^2 was approximately linear. From equation (4.9) it can be seen that this is consistent with the operation of a simple Gibrat process. Further evidence of

64   *Age-earnings profile*

this kind will be considered below. Aitchison and Brown (1957) did not mention an appropriate form for $f(t)$, although they had examined in some detail the use of a linear function, in which $f(t)$ declines steadily over age, as described in Brown (1967). This specification is discussed in section 6.1. Some empirical results are then reported in section 6.2, using both cross sectional and cohort data, and section 6.3 provides some brief examples of the tractability of the complete model.

6.1   Systematic Changes Associated with Age

The Profile of Geometric Mean Earnings

The suggestion, noted above, that the systematic component of earnings change, $f(t)$, is a steadily decreasing function of t, was based on the result that it implies a quadratic profile for geometric mean earnings with age. This is because $f(t)$ is the proportionate *change*, and must be integrated in order to obtain the profile describing the *level* of earnings at each age. A rationale for this profile has been provided by the well known basic model of the 'human capital' approach, where the proportionate change is regarded as the product of the proportion of earnings invested in 'education' during the period, d_t, and the rate of return to investment in human capital, r_t. Thus

$$f(t) = \frac{1}{m_t} \frac{dm_t}{dt} = r_t d_t \qquad (6.1)$$

Using the definition of $\mu_t = \log m_t$ and converting to discrete time, equation (6.1) can be rewritten as

$$\mu_t = \mu_{t-1} + r_t d_t$$

$$= \mu_0 + \sum_{j=1}^{t} r_j d_j \qquad (6.2)$$

where μ_0 is the arithmetic mean of log-earnings (the geometric mean of earnings) in the year of entry into the occupation.

Empirical content can be added to the model by the assumption, made by Becker (1964) and Mincer (1970), that the rate of return remains constant over age at r, while the proportion of earnings invested falls steadily with age according to

$$d_t = d_0 - gt \qquad (6.3)$$

Substituting into (6.2)

$$\mu_t = \mu_0 + rd_0 t - rg \sum_{j=1}^{t} j$$

$$= \mu_0 + r\left(d_0 - \frac{g}{2}\right)t - \frac{rg}{2}t^2 \qquad (6.4)$$

using the fact that the sum of the first n integers is

$$\sum_{j=1}^{n} j = \frac{n}{2}(n+1)$$

Thus equation (6.4) implies that geometric mean earnings are a quadratic function of age with coefficients μ_0, $\theta = r(d_0 - \frac{1}{2}g)$ and $\delta = rg/2$. Geometric mean earnings reach a maximum at age $\theta/2\delta = (d_0/g - \frac{1}{2})$. This has the interpretation that the larger the initial investment d_0, and the slower the rate at which this falls over life, the greater is the age at which income is a maximum (the slower is the rate at which $f(t)$ falls to zero). However, this rationale is somewhat *ad hoc*, and the use of the reduced form (6.4) obviously does not confirm the validity of the assumptions underlying the model. The following discussion therefore concentrates on the straightforward statistical description of systematic changes in earnings over life, based on the direct use of the quadratic

$$\mu_t = \mu_0 + \theta_t - \delta t^2 \qquad (6.5)$$

Age and the Dispersion of Earnings

Most information about the dispersion of earnings over the complete working life has necessarily been obtained using cross sectional data, and a very wide variety of data display a linear growth of σ_t^2 with t. Earlier examples include the studies by Fisher (1952, p. 83), the data from the Wharton School Survey (1957, p. 86), Lydall (1955), Aitchison and Brown (1957), data in the Department of Education and Science Survey (1966–7) for different education groups, and the series of *Family Expenditure Surveys* published annually by the Department of Employment. Morgan (1962) also observed the increasing dispersion with age, but went on to remark that 'the overall index of concentration . . . is roughly equal to the concentration of incomes at the middle of the earning life'. This raises the issue of aggregation over age groups, which will be examined in the following chapter. Nevertheless Thatcher (1971, p. 377) suggested that 'there is little observable tendency for the dispersion of earnings to increase with age'. However, it is possible that this difference may result from the restriction of his samples to those who paid at least 48 insurance contributions. For example, in the Department of Employment's *New Earnings Survey* (1975, tables 128 and 129) selected deciles of the distribution of gross weekly earnings within particular occupation and sex groups are given for a number of age groups, including only individuals whose pay was not affected by absence. In all of the professional and non-manual occupations (where sickness would have little effect) the variance of logarithms increased with age; whereas in all manual occupations there was no significant increase with age.

These and many other results suggest the wide applicability of an earnings model in which σ_t^2 increases steadily with age. However, chapter 4 has shown that this is consistent with more than one process of year-to-year earnings changes, and that some highly aggregated longitudinal data indicate small, but significant, serial correlation. As mentioned earlier it is possible that the observed aggregate serial correlation is consistent with each occupational group following a simple Gibrat process. The use of the Gibrat process must, in the absence of better data, be regarded only as a useful approximation. When the age–earnings model is used in wider economic analyses it is of course necessary to examine the sensitivity of the results to that assumption. Such analyses will be reported in Part V of this book, where the conclusions of the studies are shown not to be affected by the use of the Gibrat process as a convenient and tractable approximation.

The Form of the Distribution

In order to derive more testable predictions it is necessary to make an explicit assumption about the form of the distribution of earnings. Following Aitchison and Brown (1957), it is assumed that earnings at entry into the labour force or occupation are lognormally distributed; so y_0 is $\Lambda(y_0 \mid \mu_0, \sigma_0^2)$. Where u_t is $N(0, \sigma_u^2)$ this also implies that earnings in every age group are lognormally distributed. Then y_t is $\Lambda(y_t \mid \mu_t, \sigma_t^2)$ and

$$d\Lambda(y_t) = (2\pi\sigma_t^2 y_t^2)^{-1/2} \exp[-\tfrac{1}{2}\{(\log y_t - \mu_t)/\sigma_t\}^2]\, dy_t$$

$$y_t > 0 \qquad (6.6)$$

An example of the distribution of percentage earnings changes, using the data for 246 professional chemists mentioned in chapter 4, is shown in figure 6.1. Further analyses of similar data also indicate that the assumption of the normality of the *u*s is a reasonable approximation for present purposes.

The basic model can therefore be written as follows. The conditional distribution function of earnings, given age *t*, is

$$F(y \mid t) \text{ is } \Lambda(y \mid \mu_0 + \theta_t - \delta t^2, \sigma_0^2 + \sigma_u^2 t) \tag{6.7}$$

The lognormal distribution also has the convenient implication, noted above, that the median income is equal to the geometric mean, the logarithm of which is the mean of log-earnings. Also, the moments can be easily obtained from the moment generating

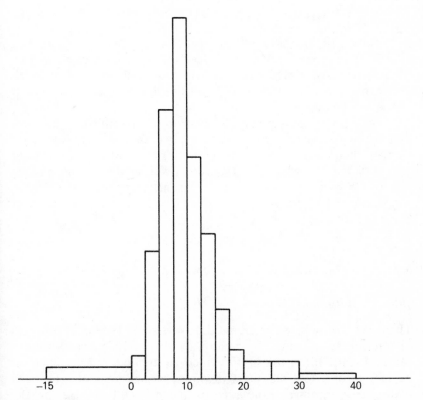

Figure 6.1   Distribution of percentage earnings changes 1971–72.

function of the normal distribution; in particular the mean and variance of earnings in each age group are given by

$$E(y_t) = \exp(\mu_t + \tfrac{1}{2}\sigma_t^2) \tag{6.8}$$

and

$$V(y_t) = E(y_t)^2\{\exp(\sigma_t^2) - 1\} \tag{6.9}$$

Equation (6.9) immediately resolves the apparent conflict between the above statements about σ_t^2 and Lydall's (1968, p. 124) remark that 'there is some doubt whether this ... increase in variance with age ... is true; and if it were true it does not seem to be very important, except for a relatively small group of highly educated people'. In fact Lydall (1968) measured $V(y_t)$ which, on expanding (6.9), is given by

$$V(y_t) = \exp\{(\sigma_0^2 + 2\mu_0) + (2\theta + \sigma_u^2)t - 2\delta t^2\}$$
$$\times \{\exp(\sigma_0^2 + \sigma_u^2 t) - 1\} \tag{6.10}$$

and is obviously concave with respect to t. The fact that increasing σ_t^2 and decreasing $V(y_t)$ are not inconsistent is easily explained by the relative nature of the former, which does not depend on levels of income and unlike the latter measure is therefore independent of the profile of μ_t.

Furthermore, comparison of equation (6.8) with (6.5) indicates that arithmetic mean income reaches a maximum $\sigma_u^2/2\delta$ years after median income attains a maximum. The tendency for higher deciles to reach a peak later than the lower deciles was noted long ago by Woytinsky (1943), and this also applies to 'between occupations' comparisons of median income; see, for example, Blaug (1970, p. 27).

6.2   Some Empirical Results

Estimation using Cross Sectional Data

The need to use cross sectional data raises the perennial problem of interpretation, since the conditions under which a cross section can be identified with a lifetime income stream are never likely to be met in practice. The most obvious factor is that of a trend in real/money earnings, although this can be handled easily in the case of constant proportionate growth, g, applied to all age groups.

This simply changes the profile of μ_t to $\mu_t = \mu_0 + (\theta + g)t - \delta t^2$, and median income increases for $g/2\delta$ years longer than otherwise.

When dealing with data relating to particular occupations much greater problems are created by mobility, since income change is often a process of successive promotion through various stages. The data necessarily relate to those remaining in the occupation so it may be difficult to interpret the results in terms of riskiness or incentives provided. For example the term σ_u^2 in the Gibrat model governs the extent to which people move within the distribution and may be thought to provide a measure of the 'riskiness' of the occupation. However, excessive risks may induce (or force) people to move to a more 'stable' occupation. Thus the resulting data, covering those left, may indicate a misleadingly low value of σ_u^2. It may however be argued that cross sectional evidence is used by individuals in forming expectations of future earnings prospects in different occupations. For example, Marshall (1890, p. 475) suggested that 'the majority assume without a further thought that the condition of each trade in their own time sufficiently indicates what it will be in the future'. Occupational choice will be examined further in section 6.3 below.

The available data are usually in the form of k independent samples at ages t_j ($j = 1, \ldots, k$) with n_j observations in each. If the earnings are first transformed by taking logarithms and the unweighted means and variances of log-earnings m_j and s_j^2 respectively, are calculated, then of course a straightforward method of estimation would be to carry out an ordinary least squares regression on the two equations

$$m_j = \mu_0 + \theta t_j - \delta t_j^2 \tag{6.11}$$

and

$$s_j^2 = \sigma_0^2 + \sigma_u^2 t_j \tag{6.12}$$

In estimating each equation separately, however, a large amount of information would be neglected, so a more efficient method is required that uses all the information in the sample. If initial estimates of σ_0^2 and σ_u^2 are obtained from an OLS regression of (6.12), the corresponding 'expected' values of σ_j^2, $\hat{\sigma}_j^2$ say, can be calculated and used to form a set of weights $w_j = n_j/\hat{\sigma}_j^2$ ($j = 1, \ldots, k$). Using these weights (proportional to the number of observations, and inversely proportional to the variance) the weighted regression of equation (6.11) can be carried out. Again, using these estimates the 'expected' values of μ_j, $\hat{\mu}_j$ say, can be calculated for each age group.

Then, using the same set of weights w_j, a weighted regression of (6.12) can be carried out, except that instead of using s_j^2 as the dependent variable the mean sum of squares

$$\frac{1}{n} \Sigma (x - \hat{\mu}_j)^2 = s_j^2 - 2\hat{\mu}_j m_j + \hat{\mu}_j^2$$

is used. This provides a second set of estimates of σ_0^2 and σ_u^2, which can be compared with the initial set. This comparison completes the *second stage* of the *first iteration* of the estimation procedure. If there is any change in the coefficients from one iteration to the next a new set of weights w_j is calculated (from the latest 'expected values' of σ_j^2) and the whole process repeated. In the cases reported below the iterative process was stopped when the percentage change in the coefficients was less than 10^{-3}, convergence usually being fairly rapid. The method described above is in fact equivalent to the maximum likelihood procedure devised by Brown (1967), and which used Fisher's 'Method of Scoring' (described in chapter 3 above).

The above method has been applied successfully to a very wide range of data. A small selection of results is given in table 6.1, using data from the *Royal Commission on Doctors' and Dentists' Remuneration* (1960). These results show that all parameter estimates are highly significantly different from zero. However, in some other cases the estimate of δ was not significantly different from zero; for example for professional chemists in 1971 the values of μ_0, θ, δ, σ_0^2 and σ_u^2 were 7.4014 (±0.0083), 0.0595 (±0.00003), 0.0009 (±0.0011), 0.0237 (±0.0012) and 0.0044 (±0.0001) respectively. A clear indication of the changing distribution of earnings with age for this group is provided by figure 6.2, which shows the cumulative distribution of earnings in each age group.

Cohort Earnings Profiles

In the previous section reference was briefly made to the problems of using cross sectional data for the analysis of age–earnings profiles. The basic problem is that comparisons among age groups at the same date show differences that arise because of the common process of ageing *and* because of differences between cohorts. Such differences may arise because of the relative sizes of

Table 6.1 Parameter estimates for selected occupations

Group	μ_0	θ	δ $(\times 10^2)$	σ_0^2	σ_u^2 $(\times 10^2)$
Surveyors	1.75	0.077	0.12	0.099	1.34
	(0.035)	(0.0043)	(0.005)	(0.01)	(0.08)
Solicitors	1.81	0.079	0.11	0.225	0.63
	(0.063)	(0.0059)	(0.005)	(0.022)	(0.10)
General medical	2.57	0.048	0.10	0.145	0.33
practitioners	(0.01)	(0.001)	(0.002)	(0.003)	(0.01)
General dental	3.0	0.032	0.10	0.199	0.70
practitioners	(0.033)	(0.004)	(0.005)	(0.012)	(0.065)
Consultants	2.99	0.056	0.10	0.068	0.34
	(0.014)	(0.002)	(0.003)	(0.003)	(0.02)
University	1.76	0.072	0.10	0.084	0.14
teachers	(0.017)	(0.002)	(0.002)	(0.003)	(0.015)
Engineers	2.14	0.038	0.05	0.034	0.70
	(0.008)	(0.0013)	(0.002)	(0.001)	(0.016)

Source: Data from the *Royal Commission on Doctors' and Dentists' Remuneration 1957-1960, Supplement to Report: Further Statistical Appendix* (1960), Cmnd 1064.

the cohorts, and the fact that there may be systematic differences between cohorts in types and levels of education.

It is important to recognize that the confounding of more than one influence on earnings changes is a problem that applies to cohort data as well as to cross sectional data. Thus, a distinction is usually made between the effects, on the earnings changes of a specified group, of three factors – *age, cohort* and *time period*. In addition to a regular ageing process, and the cohort-specific effects such as size, there may be particular events which take place over time, during the relevant period of analysis, which affect earnings growth. Factors such as major wars, inflation and productivity growth may have different effects on each age group. There may be lasting effects on certain cohorts produced by those events. The fundamental difficulty is therefore that, even with cohort data, there is an identification problem. The various effects can only be separated by imposing restrictions on the parameters of the model used. Such restrictions may be imposed after detailed analyses of other related data, giving for example some indication of the precise impact of events taking place over

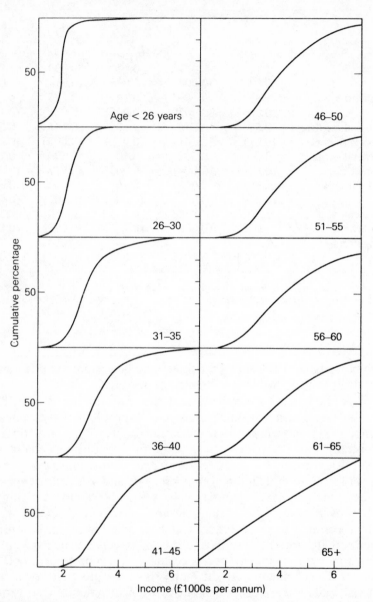

Figure 6.2 Cumulative earnings distribution for each age group (Royal Institute of Chemistry Survey, 1971).

calendar time, or of the nature of the ageing process, or of the effects of, say, cohort size on starting salaries and promotion prospects. However, in many applications it is necessary to make fairly strong assumptions such that, for example, real earnings growth is shared by all age groups alike.

This subsection does not attempt the more extensive task of trying to isolate the three basic effects mentioned above, but simply illustrates the estimation of a 'cohort' earnings profile using fairly limited data. The data used are similar to those used in chapter 4, collected by the Department of Health and Social Security in Britain. They are for three constant samples of male employees born in 1943, 1933 and 1923. Information about the annual earnings are available for the years 1963, 1968, 1971-2-3 for cohorts 1943 and 1923, and for the years 1963, 1966, 1970-1-2-3 for cohort 1933. The results are given for samples including only individuals who paid at least 48 National Insurance contributions in all of the relevant years, and therefore largely eliminate the effects of sickness and unemployment on changes in earnings.

Table 6.2 shows the values of μ_t and σ_t^2 for the three cohorts over the years from 1963 to 1973, with μ_t also given in constant prices. The profile of μ_t at 1973 prices against t for each cohort is also shown in figure 6.3, where it is clear that the experience of the three cohorts at comparable ages, but different dates, is markedly different. In particular each cohort is 'overtaken' by the succeeding cohort. The points BDF and ACE provide three points along two separate cross section profiles (the former for 1973, the latter for 1963). Direct inference from the cross section profiles would be quite misleading; in particular it would appear from the profile ACE that geometric mean earnings reach a maximum very early in working life.

It is possible, using the 16 observations in table 6.2, to estimate the parameters μ_0, θ, δ, g and h in a regression

$$\hat{\mu}_t = \hat{\mu}_0 + \hat{\theta}t - \hat{\delta}t^2 + \hat{g}d_1 + \hat{h}d_2$$

Here d_1 is a dummy variable which is unity for cohort 1933 (zero otherwise) and d_2 is a dummy variable which is unity for cohort 1923 (zero otherwise). The variable t is age minus 20 years. It is therefore assumed that not only will cohort 1943 experience similar *rates* of growth to cohorts 1933 and 1923 at comparable ages, but that the quadratic form can be extrapolated beyond the age of 50 years. The following results were obtained:

Table 6.2   Measures of logarithms of annual earnings

Group	Year	Age	μ_t	σ_t^2	μ_t at 1973 prices
Cohort 1943	1963	20	6.280	0.066	6.860
($N = 670$)	1968	25	7.038	0.079	7.422
	1971	28	7.444	0.076	7.616
	1972	29	7.586	0.111	7.684
	1973	30	7.725	0.091	7.725
Cohort 1933	1963	30	6.857	0.085	7.443
($N = 610$)	1966	33	7.130	0.094	7.590
	1970	37	7.494	0.128	7.754
	1971	38	7.592	0.129	7.764
	1972	39	7.722	0.142	7.820
	1973	40	7.843	0.130	7.843
Cohort 1923	1963	40	6.896	0.119	7.482
($N = 654$)	1968	45	7.229	0.129	7.613
	1971	48	7.533	0.140	7.705
	1972	49	7.647	0.148	7.745
	1973	50	7.773	0.128	7.773

Note: The last column is obtained using a consumer price index (*Economic Trends*, 1974). (Year, index; 1963, 0.557; 1966, 1631; 1968, 0.681; 1970, 0.771; 1971, 0.842; 1972, 0.907.)

$$\hat{\mu}_t = 6.93 + 0.0950t - 0.00146t^2 - 0.3664d_1 - 0.7411d_2$$
$$\quad\quad (0.0068)\ (0.00020)\quad\quad (0.0448)\quad (0.0723)$$

with $R^2 = 0.972$.

The parameters are all highly significantly different from zero and the goodness of fit, as measured by R^2, is very high. Although the estimated cohort profile seems to be quite different from the cross section profile, it has been shown above that the quadratic in t also fits a considerable number of cross section profiles.

The assumption used above that the different cohorts experience similar rates of growth of earnings at comparable ages was tested by adding interaction terms to the regression analysis, such as $d_1 t$. But they were not significantly different from zero. This result did not however apply to comparable data for Sweden, also used in chapter 4. The Swedish data actually cover five cohorts of males born in 1913, 1918, 1923, 1928 and 1933, and all the years 1960-

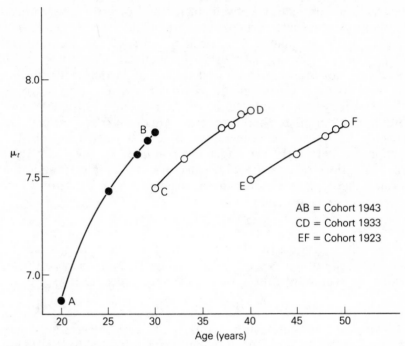

Figure 6.3 Variation in μ_t with age.

1973. The regression results in this case, for all occupations combined, were

$$\hat{\mu}_t = 8.79 + 0.118t - 0.003t^2 - 3.10d_1 - 1.99d_2$$
$$(0.02) \ (0.0027) \ (0.0001) \ (0.096) \ (0.066)$$

$$-1.13d_3 - 0.48d_4 + 0.106(td_1) + 0.078(td_2)$$
$$(0.042) \ (0.024) \ (0.0040) \ \ \ (0.0031)$$

$$+ 0.049(td_3) + 0.025(td_4) \qquad R^2 = 0.99$$
$$(0.0022) \ \ \ \ (0.0015)$$

where again t = age minus 20, and the dummy variables are as follows: $d_1 = 1$ for cohort 1913 (0 otherwise); $d_2 = 1$ for cohort 1918 (0 otherwise); $d_3 = 1$ for cohort 1923 (0 otherwise); and so on. This result shows that the slopes of the age–earnings profiles for the younger cohorts are less steep than for those of the older cohorts.

The above approach, using dummy variables (with or without interaction), provides a convenient method of estimating an age-earnings profile for a particular cohort, while acknowledging that the coefficients cannot be identified precisely as showing the effects only of age on earnings. Although sufficient information is usually not available to warrant the use of particular identifying restrictions on a general model, it is perhaps useful to illustrate the way in which results could be interpreted in different ways. Suppose, then, that there are only 'time' and 'age' effects, so specific differences between cohorts have been ruled out explicitly. Suppose also that the age effects are non-linear, as previously, and that the time effects are also quadratic. A simple formulation would then relate μ_{ts}, the mean log-earnings in age group t at calendar date s, to t and s as follows:

$$\mu_{ts} = \alpha_0 + \alpha_1 t + \alpha_2 t^2 + \beta_1 s + \beta_2 s^2$$

Now if c denotes the date of birth of a cohort, then $t = s - c$ (the cohort born in year $c = 1930$ is aged 30 in year $s = 1960$), and $s = t + c$. Substitution for s in the above specification gives

$$\mu_{t,t+c} = \alpha_0 + (\alpha_1 + \beta_1)t + (\alpha_2 + \beta_2)t^2 + \beta_1 c + 2\beta_2 ct + \beta_2 c^2$$

showing how the interaction terms, in the earlier regressions, may be interpreted in terms of non-linear 'time effects'. Furthermore, there can be differences between the *slopes* of the different cohort earnings profiles, even though the time factors need not influence each cohort differently. This is a useful result because it shows that the assumption that economic growth (a time effect) increases the real average earnings of each cohort by the same amount is therefore entirely consistent with the observation of significant interaction effects in the dummy variable regression analysis. The interactions may arise only because of the non-linearity in the time effects, rather than arising from a cohort effect. However it must again be stressed that this is only meant as an example of a possible interpretation, after very strong *a priori* restrictions have been imposed on a model. The identification of different systematic effects in practice requires more information than is currently available, and will not be pursued here.

6.3   Further Analytical Results

It has often been argued that differences in income that can be attributed to the fact that people are in different stages of the life cycle should not be regarded as 'genuine inequalities'. Thus when considering the aggregate distribution (over all ages) it is important to be able to separate the component of inequality that is determined by the age distribution alone. This is the subject of the following chapter. In behavioural problems the most obvious applications of age–earnings models are of course in life cycle models of consumption; indeed any case where expectations of future income are important. Of course, any model of the genesis of the wealth distribution must include models of saving behaviour and income over life as components. Since these subjects are much too large to be dealt with here, this section will show only how the basic unit of analysis can be extended to include the household rather than the individual, how the model can be used in a simple treatment of occupational choice, and how earnings changes affect the marginal propensity to consume.

The Inclusion of Household Size

A common procedure adopted in demand analysis is to convert household expenditure and income into 'per equivalent adult' terms, where the equivalent household 'size' is obtained as a weighted average of the number of people of each (age/sex) type in the household. If the equivalent household size, h_t, is also assumed to be lognormally distributed in each age group (using the age as that of the 'head' of the household) as $\Lambda(h_t | m_t, s_t^2)$ and the correlation between log-household income and size is r_t then the distribution of income per equivalent adult can be obtained as

$$f(h_t/y_t) = \Lambda\left(\frac{h_t}{y_t} \middle| \mu_t - m_t, \sigma_t^2 + s_t^2 - 2r_t s_t \sigma_t\right) \qquad (6.13)$$

by a straightforward application of theorem 2.4 in Aitchison and Brown (1957, p. 12). Thus the changing distribution of incomes per equivalent 'household member' is completely specified once the relevant profiles are known. Equation (6.13) represents the confluence of the two cycles of household income and size (and their interdependence) which is familiar from B. S. Rowntree's original diagrams (1899). The extension of the model to cover household income therefore presents no fundamental difficulties for its application.

Occupational Choice

The subject of occupational choice has a long and fairly consistent history in economic literature; Adam Smith's arguments are often repeated. He suggested that the relative attractiveness of occupations is determined by net advantages rather than simply pecuniary returns and that occupational choice is distorted by 'that natural confidence which every man has ... not only in his own activities, but in his own good fortune' (1776). Combined with Smith's last point is Marshall's argument that, 'if an occupation offers a few extremely high prizes, its attractiveness is increased out of all proportion to their aggregate value' (1890, p. 461).

Notwithstanding these distortions in the distribution of labour between industries, the problem is often discussed in the context of the relative 'actuarial attractiveness' of different occupations. This has been examined by Weiss (1972), who specifically limited his analysis to the aspect of decision making under risk which results from incomplete knowledge about future income prospects. The individual is assumed to maximize the expected value of utility from anticipated future income. The ultimate choice naturally depends on the attitude towards risk, as reflected in the degree of risk aversion shown by the utility function. Concerning the formation of expectations Weiss uses a similar approach to the above, and states 'the individual assumes that his income at each future age will fall within the currently observed distribution of the corresponding age group' (1972, p. 1207).

The objective function to be maximized is therefore written (1972, p. 1208) as:

$$E_T = E\left(\int_0^T e^{-rt}U(y_t)\, dt \right)$$

$$= \int e^{-rt}E\{U(y_t)\}\, dt \qquad (6.14)$$

where T is the fixed career length, r is the subjective discount rate and U is the utility function. Using the well worn function with constant relative risk aversion, $1 - a$, U is given by

$$U(y_t) = \frac{1}{a} y_t^a \qquad (6.15)$$

Then from the convenient properties of the lognormal distribution

$$E\{U(y_t)\} = \frac{1}{a} \exp(a\mu_t + \tfrac{1}{2}a^2\sigma_t^2) \tag{6.16}$$

The substitution of (6.16) into (6.14) presents obvious difficulties, and it is certainly not clear that its evaluation would give an explicit solution which is a convenient function of the subjective discount rate. This led Weiss to consider 'the special case where the parameters of the earning distributions are independent of age, and life is infinite' 1972, p. 1209). In this way Weiss obtained a simple solution for the rate of return from investment in education. This does however seem a rather artificial way of avoiding the usual problems associated with the calculation of rates of return. However, consider the basic age–earnings model summarized by equation (6.7). In this case

$$E_T = \frac{1}{a} \int \exp\{A + (B - r)t - Ct^2\}\, \mathrm{d}t \tag{6.17}$$

where $A = a\mu_0 + \tfrac{1}{2}a^2\sigma_0^2$, $B = a\theta + \tfrac{1}{2}a^2\sigma_u^2$ and $C = a\delta$.

By completing the square inside the exponent and rearranging terms, (6.17) can be simplified to give:

$$E_t = \frac{1}{a} kN(M, V^2) \tag{6.18}$$

where $k = (\pi/C)^{1/2} \exp\{A + (B - r)^2/4C\}$, and $N(M, V^2)$ denotes the Normal distribution function with parameters M and V^2, given by

$$M = (B - r)/2C \qquad \text{and} \qquad V^2 = 1/2C \tag{6.19}$$

When appropriate values for the parameters are substituted into (6.19), for any reasonable value of T the Normal integral on the right of (6.18) is close to unity. This considerably simplifies the problem, since $\log E_T$ is now only a quadratic function of r. Thus the rate of return from entering an occupation yielding a stream of expected utility of income over life of $(1/a) \exp(a\mu_t + \tfrac{1}{2}a\sigma_t^2)$ for $t = 0, \ldots, T$ over another occupation yielding a stream of $(1/a) \exp(a\mu_t^* + \tfrac{1}{2}a\sigma_t^{*2})$ is that discount rate r for which $k = k^*$. This can be seen to yield a quadratic in r, which can easily be solved.

For the very simple case where the two occupations differ only in respect of their 'riskiness', as defined in terms of σ_u^2, then r is given as the solution to

$$(B^2 - B^{*2})/4C - (B - B^*)r/2C = 0$$

so

$$r = (B + B^*)/2$$

and

$$r = a\theta + \tfrac{1}{2}a^2(\sigma_u^2 + \sigma_u^{*2}) \tag{6.20}$$

This, then provides a clear demonstration of the tractability of a simple and widely applicable model of the changing distribution of income over the life cycle when included in larger models of economic behaviour.

The Propensity to Consume

There is of course an enormous literature relating to the consumption function, which cannot possibly be reviewed here. The purpose of this subsection is simply to indicate how an age–earnings model may be used within a model of consumption. Most aggregate models of consumption are specified directly in terms of variables such as 'expected future income' where an estimating equation is obtained following the introduction of some kind of expectations adjustment mechanism in terms of lagged values. The concept of aggregate 'expected' income is not entirely clear, and indeed the so-called 'life cycle' models of consumption have made very little use of age–earnings profiles. The following considers expectations formation and aggregation explicitly.

Consider the following process of expectations formation of an individual, which can be divided into two aspects. The first concerns the changes over age in the median earnings of contemporaries, where it may be assumed that expectations of such changes are based on fairly good quality cross sectional information (the current earnings of older people). The second aspect relates to the individual's expected movement within the distribution, and the following analysis investigates the assumption that each individual expects to remain in roughly the same relative position in the distribution of his or her contemporaries. Nevertheless, because of 'stochastic' changes the actual income in any period will not be equal to expected income – although people will not immediately fully revise their previous view of their 'expected future relative position' in the distribution. The new expectation of future income will not be based exclusively on either actual (observed) income, nor on the income that was previously anticipated. It is assumed that previous expectations are adjusted by a proportion, γ, of the difference between actual income, y, and the expectation of the previous period, denoted y^*. The difference $y - y^*$ is the unanticipated component of present income.

Now suppose that current consumption is proportional to what may be called 'quasi-permanent' income y^p, which is defined as

$$y^p = \gamma(y - y^*) + y^*$$
$$= \gamma y + (1 - \gamma)y^* \qquad (6.21)$$

and y^p is a weighted average of actual and expected income. The value of y^* will of course be based on y^p_{-1} and not on y_{-1}, which will not in general be equal. This type of adjustment procedure is quite familiar, except that here expectations are not based on a simple extrapolation of past values, and it is formulated at the individual level. Since individuals can readily observe the cross sectional behaviour of median earnings with age, it is not unreasonable to write

$$y^* = y^p_{-1}(1 + \dot{m}) \qquad (6.22)$$

where $\dot{m} = (m - m_{-1})/m_{-1}$. Equations (6.21) and (6.22) can then be combined to obtain y^p in terms of actual past earnings and the profile of $\dot{m}$ with age. Continual substitution, and rearrangement, gives the result that

$$y^p = m\gamma \sum_{i=0} (1 - \gamma)^i y_{-1}/m_{-1} \qquad (6.23)$$

where summation continues back to entry into the labour force.

Equation (6.23) holds for each individual in the relevant age group. It is therefore necessary to obtain the arithmetic mean value of y^p, and this is considerably simplified by using the assumption that earnings are lognormally distributed with parameters μ_t and σ_t^2, since $E(y_t) = \exp(\mu_t + \frac{1}{2}\sigma_t^2)$ and $m_t = \exp(\mu_t)$. Taking expectations of (6.23) then gives, for each age group, t,

$$E(y^p) = m\gamma \sum (1 - \gamma)^i \exp(\frac{1}{2}\sigma_{-1}^2)$$
$$= m\gamma \sum (1 - \gamma)^{t-i} \exp(\frac{1}{2}\sigma_i^2) \qquad (6.24)$$

The concept of quasi-permanent income can easily be extended to cover expectations further into the future. The median, m, in

(6.24) would simply be replaced by an appropriately discounted sum of median earnings covering future periods from t. An explicit solution may be used following the method shown in the previous section, using equation (6.18).

A further simplification can be obtained using the linear profile of $\sigma_t^2 = \sigma_0^2 + \sigma_u^2 t$, so that after substitution into (6.24) it can be shown that

$$E(y_t^p) = \gamma s_t m_t \exp(\sigma_0^2/2) \qquad (6.25)$$

with

$$s_t = \frac{\exp\{(t+1)\sigma_u^2/2\} - (1-\gamma)^{t+1}}{\exp(\sigma_u^2/2) - (1-\gamma)}$$

For most age groups the term $(1-\gamma)^{t+1}$ may be neglected, and a further simplification results, giving

$$E(y_t^p) = [\gamma/\{1 - (1-\gamma)\exp(\sigma_u^2/2)\}]E(y_t) \qquad (6.26)$$

For illustrative purposes suppose that the consumption of each individual is proportional to quasi-permanent income, so

$$c_t = \beta y_t^p$$

The above results show that with the age–earnings model and the simple model of expectations formation, the relationship between arithmetic mean consumption and arithmetic mean observed income in each age group is also one of proportionality, but with a ratio of average consumption to average income of

$$\beta\gamma/\{1 - (1-\gamma)\exp(\sigma_u^2/2)\} \qquad (6.27)$$

The average propensity to consume therefore depends on the adjustment coefficient γ and on the variability of earnings as reflected in the value of σ_u^2. When the latter is equal to zero (equal proportionate changes for all individuals) then of course aggregation raises no difficulties, and (6.27) is simply equal to β. It can be seen that an increase in the variability of earnings lowers the observed average propensity to consume in each age group. The model therefore allows genuine life cycle aspects to be integrated into a demand model, by treating the formation of expectations explicitly in a life cycle context and by using the very tractable descriptive model of the changing distribution of earnings with age.

Further Reading

This chapter is based on Creedy (1972, 1974). The results for chemists are taken from Creedy (1974a), and the treatment of expectations and aggregate consumption is from Creedy (1975c). The cohort results for the UK are from Creedy and Hart (1979), and the Swedish results are from Creedy *et al.* (1981). The result that the ratio of income to household size is lognormally distributed, whose average is *not* equal to the ratio of average income to average household size, has also been exploited in the context of Engel curve analysis in Creedy (1973). The basic age–earnings model, along with the full details of the maximum likelihood method of estimation, are presented in Brown (1967). It has also been applied to Dutch data for various education groups by Fase (1970).

7

The Age Distribution and Aggregation

One of the many 'stylized facts' in economics which has aroused some interest is the relative stability of the personal distribution of income, in terms of the earnings measured over a fairly short period of a very broad aggregate. Another, related, 'stylized fact' is of course the apparent stability over a long period of the functional distribution. It seems ironic that in the first volume of *Econometrica* Bowley (1933) attempted to direct attention to the study of distributions in economics, whereas much more attention has been devoted to what later came to be called 'Bowley's law' of the stability of factor shares.

Pareto's emphasis on the stability of the personal distribution has already been discussed in chapter 3 of this book. Gibrat also concluded, after reviewing much continental work, that 'Dans l'état actuel de le technique statistique il est impossible d'admettre que l'inégalité des fortunes ou celles des revenus présentent une tendance vers une augmentation ou une diminution' (1931, p. 190). It is interesting in this context that although Gibrat criticized Pareto for his statements about stochastic models, Gibrat produced a stochastic model which he applied to all age groups combined and which (as shown in chapter 4) implies a continuously increasing variance of the logarithms of income. Chapter 4 showed how Kalecki's (1946) modification (by introducing Galtonian regression) produces a stable distribution, but it has been stressed that if the mobility processes are assumed to be applied to *cohorts* of individuals, then there is not necessarily any contradiction between increasing dispersion with age and stability in aggregate. This was clearly pointed out by Aitchison and Brown (1957). They suggested that the observed linear increase in the variance of the logarithms of professional earnings with age (in cross sectional data) was consistent with the Gibrat process applied to cohorts, and added

The stability of the complete distribution of professional earnings must depend on the assumption that a stream of new entrants is constantly entering the initial distributions with relatively small variances, to replace older members who are leaving, through death, retirement and other causes, the distributions with greater variances later in life (1957, p. 110).

Rutherford (1955) had independently suggested a 'new' model of income distribution in which the variance of logarithms increases linearly with age, following the Gibrat process, but geometric mean income remains constant over life (so that arithmetic mean income increases). Rutherford assumed that earnings in each year are lognormally distributed, and that birth and death rates are constant. The problem was then to examine the implications for the aggregate distribution of aggregating a set of lognormal distributions over a specified age distribution. Rutherford's analysis attracted favourable comments even from those not sympathetic to stochastic models. For example, Mincer (1970) remarked that 'Among the several stochastic models, Rutherford's is the richest in empirical predictions, providing a standard which a substantive economic model should match'. It is nevertheless necessary, as Lydall (1968, p. 124) pointed out, to extend the treatment to much more realistic assumptions concerning both the age distribution and age–earnings profiles. The purpose of this chapter is therefore to extend Rutherford's treatment to the age–earnings profiles described in chapter 6, and also to consider alternative age distributions. First, section 7.1 reviews Rutherford's 'new' model, before considering the aggregation problem more generally in section 7.2. Finally section 7.3 presents and tests a more realistic model using British data.

Before considering these analytical problems, it is worth emphasizing the need for an appropriate allowance for changes in the age distribution, even if it is only required to compare mean income in two different years for descriptive purposes. This can be shown by the following example. Using data from the Remuneration Surveys of the Royal Institute of Chemistry for all ages combined, it would appear that the geometric mean income increased by 158% between 1956 and 1971. If, however, the 1956 age distribution is used as a standard (the 1971 value calculated as if the age distribution had remained unchanged from 1956) this increase is significantly reduced to 111%.

7.1   Rutherford's 'New' Model

In the following discussion it will be more convenient to work always in terms of the distribution of log-income ($x = \log y$) rather than income. Using the notation familiar from chapters 4 and 6, Rutherford basically assumed that

$$\sigma_t^2 = \sigma_0^2 + \sigma_u^2 t$$

and

$$\mu_t = \mu \qquad \text{for all } t \tag{7.1}$$

In terms of the age distribution, Rutherford assumed that all entries occur at the beginning of working life and that 'deaths' occur at the constant proportionate rate g. The age distribution, $h(t)$, is then exponential, given by

$$h(t) = g e^{-gt} \tag{7.2}$$

Rutherford was not primarily interested in the realism of these assumptions, but in examining the form of the aggregate distribution. He was able to derive the moments of the resulting distribution. From Rutherford (1955, p. 282) these are given by

$$\mu_{2i+1} = 0 \qquad \text{and} \qquad \mu_{2i} = \frac{(2i)!}{2^i} \sum_{r=0}^{i} \sigma_0^{2r} (\sigma_u^2/g)^{i-r}/r! \tag{7.3}$$

using the conventional notation that μ_i denotes the ith moment about the arithmetic mean, and μ_i' denotes the ith moment about the origin. (Remember that these refer to the distribution of *log-income*.) Rutherford actually obtained the distribution in terms of a standard symmetrical Gram–Charlier Type-A distribution, concluding that the aggregate distribution of income was not itself lognormal (that of log-income was not Normal), despite the lognormality of every age group. However, it is instructive to compare the moments in (7.3) with those of a Normal distribution having the same mean and variance. The latter moments, denoted μ_i^N for convenience, are given by

$$\mu_{2i}^N = \frac{(2i)!}{2^i i!} (\sigma_0^2 + \sigma_u^2/g)^i = \frac{(2i)!}{2^i i!} \sum_{r=0}^{i} \binom{i}{r} \sigma_0^{2r} (\sigma_u^2/g)^{i-r} \tag{7.4}$$

Consequently the moments of the Normal distribution are less than those of the complete distribution of log-income, with the same mean and variance, by a factor

$$(i-1)\frac{(2i)!}{2^i i!}(\sigma_u^2/g)^i \tag{7.5}$$

and as σ_u^2/g will be much less than unity, expression (7.5) will rapidly become negligible as i increases. It may therefore be argued that the aggregate will not deviate greatly from lognormality, and that if the model is required for wider purposes it will not be too unreasonable to take the mean and variance (from (7.3)) of the aggregate, and treat them as parameters of a Normal distribution of log-income. However, despite the complexity of Rutherford's analysis, the problem of aggregation over ages is considerably simplified by the form of the model in equations (7.1) and (7.2); that is, the assumption of an exponential age distribution and a constant value of μ in each age group.

7.2 A More General Framework

It is useful to consider the general problem of aggregation over ages. Given the age distribution $h(t)$ and the conditional distribution of log-income in each age group, $f(x|t)$, the problem is to find the marginal distribution of log-income $f(x)$. From the relationship between marginal and conditional distributions, then

$$f(x) = \int f(x|t)h(t)\,\mathrm{d}t \tag{7.6}$$

where integration is over the range of t. In the following discussion integration is taken over the range $0 < t < \infty$, since with the forms chosen for $h(t)$ there is no need to truncate the distribution at a particular age.

There is in fact a combination of $f(x|t)$ and $h(t)$ for which the form of $f(x)$ may be obtained simply by the application of (7.6). Suppose that the age distribution is Normal, with mean and variance denoted m and s^2 respectively. Then, where $H(t)$ is the distribution function corresponding to the density $h(t)$,

$$H(t) = N(t|m, s^2) \tag{7.7}$$

Suppose, further, that the age–earnings profile is given by

$$\begin{aligned} \mu_t &= \mu_0 + \theta t \\ \sigma_t^2 &= \sigma_0^2 \end{aligned} \tag{7.8}$$

so mean log-earnings increase linearly with age and the variance of log-earnings remains constant. The stability of σ_t^2 may be regarded as arising from Galtonian regression, where the regression coefficient is equal to the correlation coefficient for all successive pairs of years. The substitution into (7.6) is more conveniently carried out in terms of the distribution function $F(x)$, since

$$F(x) = \int N(x \mid \mu_0 + \theta t, \sigma_0^2) \, dN(t \mid m, s^2)$$

$$= \int N(x - \theta t \mid \mu_0, \sigma_0^2) \, dN(bt \mid bm, b^2 s^2)$$

$$= N(x \mid \mu_0 + \theta m, \sigma_0^2 + b^2 s^2) \tag{7.9}$$

using the useful convolution property of Normal integrals; see Cramer (1946, p. 190). The result in (7.9) corresponds to the result obtained by Aitchison and Brown (1954), in the context of aggregation over occupations where every occupation has the same variance of logarithms. The usefulness of (7.9) does not of course lie in its direct applicability, but in showing the special combination of circumstances for which the convenient result holds. Deviations from linearity in μ_t and constancy in σ_t^2 lead the aggregate distribution to deviate from lognormality. Although, as argued below, the Normal distribution is often more appropriate than the exponential age distribution, neither form presents crucial problems in considering aggregation.

At this stage it is instructive to cast Rutherford's own assumptions into the form of equation (7.6) above, with the constant geometric mean income in each age group, the Gibrat mobility process and exponential age distribution. From the functional form of the Normal distribution

$$f(x \mid t) = \{2\pi(\sigma_0^2 + \sigma_u^2 t)\}^{-1/2} \exp\{-\tfrac{1}{2}(x - \mu)^2/(\sigma_0^2 + \sigma_u^2 t)\} \tag{7.10}$$

whence

$$f(x \mid t)h(t) = k_1(\lambda + t)^{-1/2} \exp\{-k_2(t^2 + \lambda t + \omega)(\lambda + t)^{-1}\}$$

$$\tag{7.11}$$

where

$$k_1 = (g^2/2\pi\sigma^2)^{1/2} \qquad\qquad k_2 = 2g$$

$$\lambda = \sigma_0^2/\sigma_u^2 \qquad\qquad\qquad \omega = \{(x - \mu)/\sigma_u\}^2/2g$$

Because of the term in $(\lambda + t)^{-1}$ the integration of (7.11) over t will obviously not give a marginal distribution of the Normal form; indeed this integration presents severe difficulties. It can also be seen that the use of the quadratic profile $\mu_t = \mu_0 + \theta t - \delta t^2$ in place of the linear profile, and of the Normal age distribution, leads to an integral of the same general form except that a fourth order polynomial in t is obtained in place of the second order $(t^2 + \lambda t + \omega)$. Indeed, all permutations of assumptions discussed here lead to the same general form of (7.11). Although it is immediately clear that the aggregate distribution would not be lognormal, even though the income distribution within each age group is lognormal, the precise extent to which it would deviate from lognormality is not so clear.

The Aggregate Mean and Variance

In view of the difficulties indicated above, it seems most appropriate to proceed by restricting the analysis to the mean and variance of the logarithms of the aggregate distribution. These are denoted M and V^2 respectively, and are in general given by

$$M = \int x \left\{ \int f(x \mid t) h(t) \, dt \right\} dx = \int \left\{ \int x f(x \mid t) \, dx \right\} h(t) \, dt \quad (7.12)$$

$$= \int \mu_t h(t) \, dt$$

and

$$V^2 = \int (x - M)^2 \left\{ \int f(x \mid t) h(t) \, dt \right\} dx$$

$$= \int \left\{ \int (x - \mu_t)^2 f(x \mid t) \, dx \right\} h(t) \, dt$$

$$+ \int (\mu_t - M)^2 \left\{ \int f(x \mid t) \, dx \right\} h(t) \, dt$$

$$= \int \sigma_t^2 h(t) \, dt + \int (\mu_t - M)^2 h(t) \, dt \quad (7.13)$$

Higher order moments can be obtained in a similar manner, but soon become rather intractable. The two parts of (7.13) correspond to the *within ages* and *between ages* components of the overall variation. It is clear that the statement made by Morgan (1962), that the overall index of concentration is approximately equal to that of incomes at the middle of earning life (quoted in the previous chapter), will not in general be true. Since Rutherford assumed a constant geometric mean income his analysis was considerably simplified as only the *within ages* component had to be considered. The following section thus examines the forms taken by (7.12) and (7.13) when a more realistic age–earnings profile is used.

7.3   A More Realistic Model

Retaining Rutherford's assumption of the exponential age distribution, the result of using a quadratic profile $\mu_t = \mu_0 + \theta t - \delta t^2$ (discussed in chapter 6) can be seen as follows. First, substitute the quadratic into (7.12) whence

$$M = g \int e^{-gt}(\mu_0 + \theta t - \delta t^2)\, dt \tag{7.14}$$

This can be evaluated using the general result, obtained by integrating by parts, that

$$I(n) = \int t^n e^{-gt} = n!/g^{n+1} \tag{7.15}$$

so

$$M = \mu_0 + \theta/g - 2\delta/g^2 \tag{7.16}$$

There is a clear intuitive explanation for the result shown in equation (7.16), since the assumption of an exponential age distribution arising from a constant exit rate implies that the average length of 'life' in the labour force is $1/g$. Similarly the *within ages* component of V^2 is easily seen to be $\sigma_0^2 + \sigma_u^2/g$. The *between ages* component is more cumbersome, and is given by

$$g \int e^{-gt}(\mu_0 + \theta t - \delta t^2 - M)^2\, dt$$

writing $\mu_0 - M = 2\delta/g^2 - \theta/g = z$, say, and using (7.15) this is g multiplied by

$$z^2 I(0) + 2z\theta I(1) + (\theta^2 - 2\delta z)I(2) - 2\delta\theta I(3) + \delta^2 I(4)$$

After some simplification, this gives

$$V^2 = (\sigma_0^2 + \sigma_u^2/g) + g^4(20\delta^2 - 8\delta\theta g + \theta^2 g^2) \tag{7.17}$$

Thus (7.17) provides a convenient interpretation of the variance of log-income of the complete distribution in terms of the changing distribution of income with age and the age structure of the working population. Equations (7.16) and 71.17) should be compared with Rutherford (1955, p. 282).

A Normal Age Distribution and Tests of the Model

If 'entries' are allowed at different ages, as in the case of the age distribution of 'heads' of households or an occupation that may cover several categories of work where each requires different levels or types of skill, then the exponential distribution may no longer be applicable. With the Normal age distribution used earlier, the value of M is given by

$$M = \int (\mu_0 + \theta t - \delta t^2) \, dN(t \mid m, s^2)$$

$$M = \mu_0 + \theta m - \delta(s^2 + m^2) \tag{7.18}$$

This is obtained using the well known result that $\mu_2' = \mu_2 + \mu_1'^2$, where the prime indicates moments about the origin.

The *within ages* component of V^2 is easily seen to be $\sigma_0^2 + \sigma_u^2 m$, while the *between ages* component is rather more cumbersome to derive. For this reason the derivation is not shown here. Where, as before, z is defined as the difference between μ_0 and M, then

$$V^2 = \sigma_0^2 + \sigma_u^2 m - z^2 + \theta^2(s^2 + m^2) + \delta(3s^2 + m^2)(z - \theta m)$$

and on substitution for $z = \delta(s^2 + m^2) - \theta m$, this simplifies further to

$$V^2 = \sigma_0^2 + \sigma_u^2 m + \theta^2 s^2 + 2\delta^2 s^2(s^2 + m^2) - 4\delta\theta m^2 \tag{7.19}$$

Again equations (7.18) and (7.19) decompose the overall mean and variance of log-income into their 'demographic' components. The effect of changes in the age distribution on the overall variance of log-income can therefore easily be analysed, since

$$\frac{dV^2}{dm} = \sigma_u^2 + 4\delta m(\delta s^2 - 2\theta)$$

$$\frac{dV^2}{ds^2} = \theta^2 + 2\delta^2(s^2 + m^2) \tag{7.20}$$

so an increase in s^2 will always increase V^2 (not surprisingly) whereas an increase in the arithmetic mean age will only increase V^2 if $\delta s^2 > 2\theta$.

A Test of the Model

It was decided to test the appropriateness of the model as a whole by using estimates of the parameters m, s^2, δ, θ, and so on, and substituting these into equations (7.18) and (7.19) in order to obtain 'expected values' of M^2 and V^2. These were then compared with the actual values obtained from aggregate data, and which of course are also subject to sampling errors.

Although the model would apply to a large variety of occupations the data used here are taken from the *Family Expenditure Surveys* for households from 1956 to 1971 inclusive. The method of estimation used to obtain the parameters of the income model has been described in chapter 6, and the estimates are given in table 7.1. The parameters (except for μ_0 and σ_u^2) have remained fairly stable throughout the period although the estimates of δ

Table 7.1   Parameters of the age-income profiles model

Year	μ_0	δ	θ	σ_0^2*	σ_u^2
1965	1.249	0.0011	0.0950	−0.0330	0.0066
	(0.099)	(0.0043)	(0.00004)	(0.0136)	(0.0003)
1966	1.854	0.00085	0.0729	−0.0258	0.0069
	(0.0832)	(0.0037)	(0.00004)	(0.0133)	(0.0003)
1967	1.918	0.00083	0.0698	−0.0154	0.0064
	(0.0544)	(0.0024)	(0.00003)	(0.0087)	(0.0002)
1968	2.1964	0.00075	0.0622	−0.0177	0.0066
	(0.0531)	(0.0023)	(0.00002)	(0.0089)	(0.0002)
1969	2.343	0.00071	0.0561	0.0306	0.0045
	(0.0543)	(0.0024)	(0.00002)	(0.0082)	(0.0002)
1970	2.233	0.00081	0.0673	0.0333	0.0058
	(0.0561)	(0.0024)	(0.00002)	(0.0101)	(0.0002)
1971	2.211	0.00086	0.0723	0.0170	0.0063
	(0.0532)	(0.0023)	(0.00002)	(0.0095)	(0.0002)

*t is measured from birth, so the values of σ_0^2 are the intercepts of σ_t^2 on the axis, when $t = 0$; this explains why some values are shown as negative.
Standard errors are shown in parentheses immediately underneath parameter estimates.
(*Source: Family Expenditure Surveys* 1965–1971.)

are not significantly different from zero, indicating little deviation from a straight line profile for μ_t with t. These must be combined with the estimates of m and s, given in table 7.2, which indicate that while m has remained fairly stable over the period the variance s^2 has increased somewhat. The 'actual' and 'estimated' values of M and V^2 are also shown in table 7.2, and appear to be fairly encouraging in most cases. If it is required to derive the effect of certain demographic factors on the aggregate distribution, either for its own sake or as part of a larger model, then it is argued that equations (7.18) and (7.19) will give fairly good approximations to M and V^2.

The above discussion has been concerned with the problem of obtaining the aggregate distribution of income over age groups, where there are important systematic differences in the income distribution of each age group. It has been shown that if proportionate income changes from one year to the next are not systematically correlated with the current level of income, so that the dispersion of incomes increases with age, then stability of the complete distribution is produced by simple 'birth–death' processes.

Using a widely applicable model of the changing distribution of income over life, formulae for the mean and variance of the aggregate distribution of log-income have been obtained which provide a decomposition of these measures into their 'demographic

Table 7.2 Parameters of aggregate distributions

| | Age of head of household | | Income distributions | | | |
| | | | Actual | | Estimated | |
Year	m	s^2	M	V^2	M	V^2
1965	50.54	223.72	3.02	0.41	3.27	0.41
1966	49.90	219.79	3.12	0.41	3.19	0.42
1967	50.30	246.20	3.16	0.41	3.13	0.44
1968	50.46	254.27	3.21	0.42	3.23	0.43
1969	50.77	264.22	3.27	0.44	3.20	0.40
1970	50.29	271.59	3.35	0.47	3.35	0.48
1971	50.50	274.04	3.43	0.49	3.43	0.50

Note: Age is measured in years from birth and income is measured in pounds per week.
(*Source*: *Family Expenditure Surveys* 1965–1971.)

components'. The effect of changes in these factors (the age distribution and the characteristics of age–income profiles) on the aggregate distribution can then easily be analysed.

It has been shown that if income in each age group is assumed to be lognormally distributed then this is not in general consistent with the use of a lognormal distribution to describe the aggregate distribution. Nevertheless the departure from lognormality would not usually be expected to be large. It is therefore suggested that the aggregate distribution could be approximated by the lognormal form $\Lambda(y|M, V^2)$, especially where the integration of the distribution into larger models will depend on its tractability in them. It is perhaps worth noting here that the task is not simply that of finding a functional form that provides the closest approximation to the data (however defined). Other relevant criteria have been discussed at greater length by Aitchison and Brown (1954, 1957, p. 108).

The next section turns to the analysis of a rather different type of aggregation problem, that of adding incomes over a number of consecutive periods. It will again be seen that no simple statements about the distribution of a sum of incomes can be made, but some more limited results can be obtained which are nevertheless useful.

Further Reading

This chapter is based on Creedy (1972, 1975). Other than the often-cited paper of Rutherford (1955), it is difficult to find serious studies of the aggregation problem raised in this chapter, although many authors have commented briefly on the issue. However, using a completely different approach, Mookherjee and Shorrocks (1982) provide an analysis of UK inequality over time, allowing for changes in the age distribution.

Part V
The Time Period and the Distribution of Earnings

8

Earnings Mobility and the Time Period of Analysis

The fact that the measured inequality of earnings may depend crucially on the length of time over which the earnings are measured has long been recognized. The distributions of hourly, weekly or annual earnings, or of earnings measured over several years or indeed over the complete life cycle, cannot be expected to have similar characteristics. The need for an examination of the relationships among alternative distributions has been stressed by the *Royal Commission on the Distribution of Income and Wealth* (1975, Report no. 1, p. 147) which stated that 'it is important ... to know what differences exist between the incomes of individuals over their lifetimes, or at least over longer periods than single years, so that their mobility within the distribution can be seen'. This quotation also indicates the strong connection between earnings mobility and the effect of measuring earnings over longer periods. Comparisons are also complicated by the fact that the dispersion of a sum of incomes depends not only on the extent to which changes in relative earnings occur, but also on the general growth of average earnings over the period.

One general approach to mobility measurement has been proposed by Shorrocks (1976), who has suggested a measure based on a normalization of measured inequality over several periods. He uses an index of 'rigidity', R, defined as the ratio of the measure of inequality over several periods to a weighted average of the inequality measures for each period taken separately. The weight for each period is the proportion of total earning that accrues in that period; that is, the ratio of the arithmetic mean for the period to the arithmetic mean of all periods combined. He then defines mobility, M, as $1 - R$. This differs from the mobility measures used in Part III, which reflect the *way* in which people move within the earnings distribution. Shorrocks' measure M reflects the extent to which 'equality' occurs as the length of the time period is extended, which is a somewhat different concept.

For the convenient case where both the mean and the inequality of income within each period are constant, Shorrocks' measure is simply the proportional reduction in the inequality measure resulting from combining several years' incomes rather than using only one year's income. For example, in the case of the coefficient of variation over two years, the appropriate measure can be shown to be $1 - \{(1 + \rho)/2\}^{1/2}$; where ρ is the correlation coefficient between incomes in the two years. Notice that when $\rho = 1, M = 0$, but when $\rho = 0, M = 1 - 1/\sqrt{2}$. This example, while unrealistically simple, also illustrates that if a certain policy reduces the correlation between incomes in consecutive years (and thereby increases mobility in the sense used earlier) the resulting value of M will depend on the initial value of ρ since $\mathrm{d}M/\mathrm{d}\rho = -\frac{1}{2}\{2(1+\rho)\}^{-1/2}$. This may be interpreted as stating that the achievement of a given increase in mobility is more difficult at lower levels of mobility.

It was pointed out in chapter 4 that until the data used in that chapter were available, the only studies using data for more than one year in Britain were by Vandome (1958) and Prest and Stark (1967), although that by Vandome was the only one that used individual observations. The second study used information on grouped income classes from the 105th Inland Revenue *Report*. This gave the average percentage change in earnings between 1958 and 1959, by income group occupied in 1958. More data have of course been available in the United States, and brief descriptive studies of the effect of changing the accounting period include Hanna (1948), Kuznets (1950), Kravis (1962), and more recently Benus and Morgan (1974), Cohen *et al.* (1974) and Steinberg (1977). These studies have not attempted to examine the general problem of adding incomes over several time periods. Section 8.1 below uses the longitudinal data for Britain, described in chapter 4, to describe the extent to which measured inequality changes as the time period changes. Section 8.2 then provides a more formal analysis of the behaviour of the coefficient of variation of earnings.

8.1   Earnings over Several Years

This section compares alternative measures of location and dispersion for distributions of earnings over several consecutive years.

Although the main interest here is in the effect of different time, or accounting, periods on the measured dispersion of earnings, the corresponding values of the arithmetic and geometric means are presented (denoted by $\bar{y}$ and G respectively). Some additional measures of inequality may of course be derived from these measures of location (as noted in chapter 2 above). Since no single

Table 8.1 Comparison of alternative distributions

Summary measure	1971	1972	1973	71 + 72	72 + 73	71 + 72 + 73
Cohort 1943 $N = 1346$						
$\bar{y}$	1657	1941	2215	3598	4156	5813
G	1516	1776	2010	3341	3867	5443
η	0.382	0.397	0.411	0.376	0.386	0.371
σ^2	0.240	0.256	0.254	0.185	0.162	0.146
$I(1.2)$	0.109	0.112	0.117	0.090	0.085	0.078
$I(1.6)$	0.175	0.213	0.182	0.141	0.121	0.110
$I(2.0)$	0.286	0.477	0.283	0.237	0.166	0.150
Cohort 1933 $N = 1157$						
$\bar{y}$	1918	2225	2468	4142	4692	6610
G	1707	2024	2223	3787	4303	6078
η	0.477	0.461	0.465	0.454	0.450	0.445
σ^2	0.303	0.203	0.243	0.185	0.177	0.170
$I(1.2)$	0.140	0.109	0.122	0.103	0.099	0.096
$I(1.6)$	0.224	0.150	0.177	0.138	0.134	0.129
$I(2.0)$	0.377	0.199	0.253	0.177	0.172	0.165
Cohort 1923 $N = 1252$						
$\bar{y}$	1840	2073	2303	3914	4377	6217
G	1645	1850	2082	3548	3987	5680
η	0.531	0.524	0.492	0.517	0.495	0.496
σ^2	0.247	0.259	0.222	0.193	0.184	0.174
$I(1.2)$	0.129	0.132	0.117	0.111	0.106	0.102
$I(1.6)$	0.184	0.191	0.167	0.147	0.140	0.134
$I(2.0)$	0.265	0.277	0.243	0.188	0.179	0.167

inequality measure can claim to be unambiguously superior, a number of alternatives are reported. The first two are the familiar coefficient of variation, η, and the variance of logarithms, σ^2. Finally several values of Atkinson's measure were obtained. This is denoted $I(\epsilon)$, where ϵ is the 'inequality aversion' parameter, discussed in chapter 2.

The values of the various measures calculated from the DHSS data are presented in table 8.1. These samples do not correspond precisely to those used in chapter 4, since they include all individuals whose earnings records were complete (irrespective of their labour market experience), and are therefore larger samples. First, it can be seen that the ranking of the different distributions by alternative measures of inequality is fairly consistent. In the few cases where rankings are different the measures are very close. Furthermore the inequality of the two- and three-year distributions is lower than in *all* of the component years for all measures and cohorts (with the single exceptions of the coefficients of variation for cohort 1923). This general result is also obtained by Hanna (1948, p. 254) for values of η over similar time periods, by Benus and Morgan (1974, p. 215) for the Gini measure, and by Vandome (1958, p. 88) for the Lorenz measure. This is not in fact a necessary consequence of aggregation over time, although the measure for combined periods cannot exceed that of any single year, as shown in section 8.2 below. Results were also obtained for the discounted sum of earnings, using alternative discount rates, but the time period is too short to affect any of the inequality measures.

From table 8.1 is can be seen that the percentage reduction in inequality that results from adding two years, when compared with inequality in one year, is well over 20 per cent (not counting the case of η). When a third year is added, however, the subsequent reduction (three years compared with two) is noticeably less. This observation raises the general question of a possible convergence in the measures of inequality as the number of time periods is increased. This problem is also examined in section 8.2.

8.2   A Formal Analysis

This section provides a more formal analysis of the implications, for the coefficient of variation, of lengthening the period of time over which earnings are measured. In view of the use made throughout this book of the lognormal distribution as a convenient approximation, it may seem more appropriate to investigate directly the distribution of the sum of lognormal variates. However, this is rather intractable because the product, not the sum, of lognormal variates is itself lognormally distributed. Suppose that Y_i represents the sum of earnings of individual i from t to T, and let $x_{it} = \log y_{it}$. Then

$$Y_i = \sum_{j=t}^{T} y_{ij} = \Sigma \exp(x_{ij})$$

$$= (T - t) + \sum_j x_{ij} + \tfrac{1}{2} \sum_j x_{ij}^2 + \tfrac{1}{6} \sum_j x_{ij}^3 + \ldots \qquad (8.1)$$

If x_i is Normally distributed in each period, the examination of (8.1) requires knowledge of the distribution, or at least the moments, of powers of Normal variates. An examination of Haldane's (1942) formulae shows that the approach is unlikely to yield practicable results. The treatment of two correlated lognormal variates has been given by Hamdan (1971), and also indicates the intractability of the present problem. The present approach therefore follows that of chapter 7 (concerning aggregation over age distributions) by examining the mean and variance explicitly, but here it is obviously necessary to work in terms of earnings rather than log-earnings. The assumption of lognormality within each age group will nevertheless be maintained in much of what follows. It has not been possible to obtain corresponding results for other measures of dispersion. This situation may be contrasted with the problem faced by Galton in examining the distribution of heights of individuals, where each person's height is determined by a sum of the lengths of many different bones. Galton was dealing with a sum of Normal variates and, as he observed, 'The beautiful regularity in the statures of a population, wherever they are statistically marshalled in the order of their heights, is due to the number of variable and quasi-independent elements of which stature is the sum' (1889, p. 85).

The Coefficient of Variation

Let the coefficient of variation of earnings of a constant group of individuals in period t be denoted η_t. This is of course obtained

102 Time period and distribution of earnings

using $\eta_t^2 = s_t^2/\bar{y}_t^2$, where $\bar{y}_t$ and s_t^2 denote the arithmetic mean and variance of the group at t. If Y_i is the ith individual's sum of earnings from 1 to T, then

$$Y_i = \sum_{t=1}^{T} y_{it}$$

and the mean and variance of earnings measured over the longer period, $E(Y)$ and $V(Y)$, are respectively

$$E(Y) = E\left(\sum_t y_{it}\right) = \sum_t \bar{y}_t \qquad (8.2)$$

$$V(Y) = \sum_{t=1}^{T} s_t^2 + 2 \sum_{j=1}^{T-1} \sum_{k=j+1}^{T} s_{jk} \qquad (8.3)$$

where s_{jk} denotes the covariance of earnings in periods j and k. If the coefficient of variation of the long period measure of earnings is denoted $\eta_{(T)}$, then

$$\eta_{(T)}^2 = V(Y)/E(Y)^2 \qquad (8.4)$$

The formal analysis of $\eta_{(T)}^2$ therefore requires further details about the values of s_{jk}, which in turn depend directly on the process of relative earnings mobility. This chapter concentrates on the implications of the Gibrat process described in chapter 4, but one general result can first be stated, using as an example the case of only two periods. If ρ denotes the correlation coefficient between earnings in the two periods, then since $s_{12} = \rho s_1 s_2$, equations (8.3) and (8.4) give

$$\eta_{(2)}^2 = (\bar{y}_1^2\eta_1^2 + \bar{y}_2^2\eta_2^2 + 2\rho\bar{y}_1\bar{y}_2\eta_1\eta_2)/(\bar{y}_1 + \bar{y}_2)^2 \qquad (8.5)$$

Now define the weighted average η^*, where

$$\eta^{*2} = (\bar{y}_1\eta_1^2 + \bar{y}_2\eta_2^2)/(\bar{y}_1 + \bar{y}_2) \qquad (8.6)$$

Subtracting (8.6) from (8.5) and rearranging gives

$$\eta_{(2)}^2 - \eta^{*2} = -\{(\eta_1 - \eta_2)^2 + 2\eta_1\eta_2(1-\rho)\}\,\bar{y}_1\bar{y}_2/(\bar{y}_1 + \bar{y}_2)^2 \qquad (8.7)$$

and because every term in (8.7) is positive, $\eta_{(2)}^2$ is always less than the weighted average η^{*2}. This shows that $\eta_{(2)}$ cannot exceed the highest value of η_t. However, it is possible for $\eta_{(2)}$ to be lower than *both* η_1 and η_2, depending on the ratios η_1/η_2, $\bar{y}_1/\bar{y}_2$ and ρ. By a process of aggregating over a number of sub-periods, this result demonstrates that the inequality of lifetime earnings cannot exceed the largest value of the coefficient of variation in any age group, although it may be lower than in every single year. The estimates of the following chapter show however that the inequality of lifetime earnings is generally somewhere between the highest and lowest annual values.

Implications of the Gibrat Process

Consider the problem of finding the covariance, s_{jk}, between earnings in years j and k. Now by definition

$$s_{jk} = E(y_j y_k) - E(y_j) E(y_k) \tag{8.8}$$

and since the last term in (8.8) is just $\bar{y}_j \bar{y}_k$, it remains to derive only the first term. Using the assumption that earnings in each group are lognormally distributed as $\Lambda(y_j | \mu_j, \sigma_j^2)$, and with $x = \log y$, then $E(y_j y_k) = E\{\exp(x_j + x_k)\}$. The problem is therefore equivalent to finding the *arithmetic mean* of a lognormal variate with mean of logarithms $\mu_j + \mu_k$ and variance of logarithms $V(x_j + x_k)$. Fase (1971) has shown that, for $k > j$,

$$V(x_j + x_k) = 3\sigma_j^2 + \sigma_k^2 \tag{8.9}$$

Thus using the result for a lognormal distribution that $E(y) = \exp(\mu + \frac{1}{2}\sigma^2)$, the mean of $x_j + x_k$ is given, again for $k > j$, by

$$E\{\exp(x_j + x_k)\} = \exp\{\mu_j + \mu_k + \frac{1}{2}(3\sigma_j^2 + \sigma_k^2)\}$$

$$= \bar{y}_j \bar{y}_k \exp(\sigma_j^2) \tag{8.10}$$

since $\bar{y}_j = E(y_j)$. Using the further result, given by Aitchison and Brown (1957, p. 8) that $\eta^2 = \exp(\sigma^2) - 1$, the substitution of (8.10) into (8.8) then gives, given $k > j$,

$$s_{jk} = \bar{y}_j \bar{y}_k \eta_j^2 \tag{8.11}$$

It is instructive to consider the special case where $\bar{y}_j = \bar{y}$, for all j; that is, where the arithmetic mean is the same in every period. Here the subsitution into (8.4), using (8.3) and (8.11), gives

$$\eta_{(T)}^2 = 2 \sum_{t=1}^{T} (T + \tfrac{1}{2} - t) \eta_t^2 / T^2 \tag{8.12}$$

Using this result the transformation between $\eta^2_{(T)}$ and η^2_t can be written in the following matrix form:

$$
\begin{bmatrix} \eta^2_{(1)} \\ \eta^2_{(2)} \\ \eta^2_{(3)} \\ \eta^2_{(4)} \\ \vdots \end{bmatrix} = \begin{bmatrix} 1 & 0 & 0 & 0 & \ldots \\ 3 & 1 & 0 & 0 & \ldots \\ 5 & 3 & 1 & 0 & \ldots \\ 7 & 5 & 3 & 1 & \ldots \\ \vdots & \vdots & \vdots & \vdots & \end{bmatrix} \begin{bmatrix} \eta^2_1 \\ \eta^2_2 \\ \eta^2_3 \\ \eta^2_4 \\ \vdots \end{bmatrix} \tag{8.13}
$$

If the matrix on the right-hand side of (8.13) is denoted A, and if

$$
L = \begin{bmatrix} 0 & 0 & 0 & 0 & \ldots \\ 1 & 0 & 0 & 0 & \ldots \\ 0 & 1 & 0 & 0 & \ldots \\ 0 & 0 & 1 & 0 & \ldots \\ \vdots & \vdots & \vdots & \vdots & \end{bmatrix}
$$

then it can be seen that $A = I + 3L + 5L^2 + 7L^3 + 9L^4 + \ldots$ and

$$
A^{-1} = \begin{bmatrix} 1 & 0 & 0 & 0 & \ldots \\ -3 & 1 & 0 & 0 & \ldots \\ 4 & -3 & 1 & 0 & \ldots \\ -4 & 4 & -3 & 1 & \ldots \\ \vdots & \vdots & \vdots & \vdots & \end{bmatrix}
$$

which can also be expressed as a polynomial involving the square matrix, L, with coefficients, after the second, alternating between 4 and -4. Thus for $T > 2$, these results show that

$$
\eta^2_T = \eta^2_{(T)} - 3\eta^2_{(T-1)} + 4 \sum_{t=1}^{T-2} (-1)^{T+t} \eta^2_{(t)} \tag{8.14}
$$

The Question of Convergence

The above results help to provide some insight into the question of whether or not the measure of dispersion approaches a stable value as the length of time, over which earnings are measured, increases. A number of earlier studies have suggested that convergence to a stable value is 'likely' after only a few years; these studies include Hanna (1948, p. 214), Vandome (1958, p. 88) and Benus and

Morgan (1974, p. 216). If this were true then considerable savings could be made in attempting to obtain information about the inequality of earnings over as long a period as the working life.

Convergence can however be seen to depend on inequality within each period remaining constant, a point most clearly indicated by Vandome (1958, p. 89). In the context of the life cycle of earnings it has been seen in Part IV that a steady increase in σ_t^2 is a common characteristic of many groups. In the Gibrat case discussed in the previous subsection, this implies a linear increase in σ_t^2 but an exponential increase in $\eta_t^2 = \exp(\sigma_t^2) - 1$. Equation (8.12) shows that $\eta_{(T)}^2$ is a weighted average of separate periods' η_t^2s, with the weights declining arithmetically as t increases. This combination of exponential growth of the η_t^2s with arithmetic weights ensures that $\eta_{(T)}^2$ does not approach a stable limit as T increases. The dispersion of earnings over the complete working life therefore needs to be examined in more detail, and this is the subject to the following chapter.

Further Reading

This chapter is based on Creedy (1979). Other than the empirical studies mentioned in the text, this aggregation problem has received surprisingly little attention. However, Shorrocks (1978a, 1981) has used the effects of different accounting periods to provide a measure of mobility. His approach has been used by Markandya (1982) to examine mobility among broad occupational groups.

9

The Distribution of Lifetime Earnings

The previous chapter concentrated on the effect on a measure of dispersion of lengthening the period of time over which earnings are measured. The purpose of the present chapter is to concentrate more closely on the distribution of *lifetime* earnings, including measures of average earnings as well as their dispersion. Section 9.1 suggests how lifetime earnings in different occupations may be compared, while sections 9.2 and 9.3 show how the dispersion of earnings may be estimated for different mobility processes.

The estimation of some measure of average lifetime earnings has attracted much more attention in the past than the problem of examining the dispersion of lifetime earnings. The main concern of recent work has been to estimate the private and social returns to investment in education, or human capital, and in determining compensation for personal injury or death. In fact the practice of compensation can be traced to Anglo-Saxon times, when the 'wer' or 'wergild' was the amount that had to be paid to a man's relatives by his murderer, although this amount was mainly determined by social prestige (see Lipson, 1949, pp. 19, 29).

The earlier attempts to measure lifetime earnings were made for quite different reasons from those mentioned above. First, the pioneering calculations of Sir William Petty were made to obtain a measure of the 'wealth of the nation' which included human capital. He subtracted the sum of rent and profits from total annual expenditure. This figure was multiplied by 20, based on the assumption of 'the mass of mankind being worth twenty years purchase', and then divided by the total population to give 'the value of each head of man, woman and child'.

Secondly, Farr (1853) was concerned with devising a system of taxation that he thought would be more equitable than the existing system. This involved the taxation of 'human capital' comparable with other property taxes, rather than the straightforward taxation of current income. Farr was probably the first person to use income data classified by age, and found that the 'labouring classes' reached maximum income at the average age of 25 years. The taxation of 'potential' future income, or an average of earnings over a long period, has been discussed many times since Farr. The subject of income averaging for tax purposes is examined in more detail in chapter 10.

A third stimulus to measuring the 'value of man' was provided by the need to measure the 'indirect' costs of war. Notable examples here include Giffen (1880), Nicholson (1891), Barriol (1910), Crammond (1915) and Boag (1916). The concept of 'human capital' had of course been firmly established long before the more recent fashion.

Fourthly, building on Farr's work, Dublin and Lotka (1930) provided the first really 'scientific' estimates of 'the value of man as a wage earner'. Their detailed studies arose out of insurance work to provide a guide both for insurance agents and for the customer to indicate 'what his responsibility really is'.

Finally, there is the huge study by Clark (1937) which arose out of his interest in manpower planning. He complained of 'the misplaced emphasis, while spending ... chapters discussing hourly wage rates, to exclude life earnings entirely'. Mention should again be made of the study by Friedman and Kuznets (1954). They used income profiles for different professions to demonstrate the existence of non-competing groups, suggesting that 'Practically all professional workers are making more than their competitive worth would justify'.

9.1 Alternative Measures of Lifetime Earnings

Each of the approaches mentioned above will clearly involve the use of a different measure of lifetime earnings. However, the concept of the present value of an income stream is fundamental. The present section concentrates on the problem of *comparisons* among different income streams. It has often been pointed out that a comparison of average lifetime earnings between two occupations (education groups, or regions) will give a different impression from a simple comparison of average earnings in any year (for example in the year for which average earnings in each occupation are at a maximum). The point was clearly made in the third report of the *Royal Commission on the Distribution of Income and Wealth* (1976, p. 258). Weisbrod (1962) earlier compared ratios of mean earnings in different states of the US (which depend on factors such as the age distribution in each state) with ratios of average lifetime earnings and found the former larger than the latter in all cases. He did not consider the dispersion of lifetime earnings, however.

The emphasis of the present section is that the arithmetic mean of lifetime earnings is not necessarily the best measure to use for comparison purposes, despite its widespread use. It is used in virtually all human capital studies, and also in most discussions of dual labour markets. For example Bosanquet and Doeringer (1973) compared occupations using only average profiles, stating that 'for each education level, males earn more on average than females at the start of their careers, and the gap is larger in the higher age groups'. This is used as 'evidence' for the existence of dual labour markets, despite the fact that there are significant *overlaps* among the relevant distributions.

The Use of the Arithmetic Mean

The popularity of the arithmetic mean is easily explained by its ease of calculation, given only arithmetic mean earnings within a number of age groups in a cross section (although of course these data may first be adjusted for productivity growth or inflation). This in turn is simply because the arithmetic mean of discounted lifetime earnings is equivalent to the discounted value of arithmetic mean earnings in each age group. Define the following:

y_{it} = earnings of individual i in year t

c_t = the discount factor appropriate to year t

Y_{it} = person i's discounted value of earnings from 1 to T. Then

$$Y_i = \sum_{t=1}^{T} c_t y_{it}$$

and

$$E(Y) = \Sigma c_t E(y_t) \tag{9.1}$$

This convenient property could clearly not be expected to hold for other measures of location. Thus the discounted value of median earnings in each age group would not in general be equal to the median value in the distribution of discounted lifetime earnings.

An objection to the use of the arithmetic mean in this context is that the distribution of lifetime earnings would be expected to be highly skewed. Thus the mean and the variance of the distribution are not independent and comparisons could be highly misleading. The problem here is that, without actual cohort data, it is not possible to obtain alternative conventional measures such as the median. This is because, as explained in chapter 8, the functional form of the distribution cannot be obtained explicitly even if the distribution within each age group, and the way in which earnings change from year to year, are known.

A further objection to such comparisons is that they actually provide very little information about relative prospects in different occupations. Much more information would ideally be required by anyone considering occupational choice. An alternative procedure is therefore suggested below.

Alternative Measures of Location

It seems desirable to provide summaries of 'lifetime earnings' in different occupations which provide more information about prospects than the arithmetic mean. Examples of age–earnings profiles for two professions are shown in figure 9.1, where the profiles for the median and lower and upper quartile at each age are shown in addition to the arithmetic mean. These profiles are based on the estimates reported in chapter 6. The different shapes of the profiles in the two professions are clearly shown. For example, there is a much greater difference between the mean and the median profiles for surveyors than for general medical practitioners.

Now the value of $E(Y)$ can be interpreted as the discounted earnings of an individual who receives the arithmetic mean earnings of his contemporaries in each year of his working life. This interpretation suggests that it may also be of interest to examine the life earnings of someone who is assumed to remain in a particular quantile of the distribution of his contemporaries. For example, a further range of comparisons can be made between individuals with different earning profiles in each occupation. It

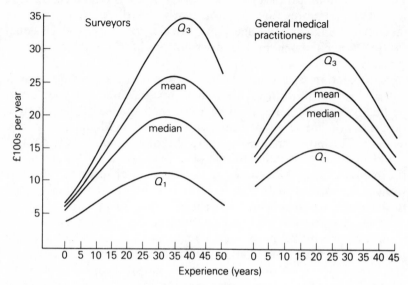

Figure 9.1   Examples of age–earnings profiles.

must of course be recognized that in practice individuals do move among quantiles of the distribution, but it is suggested that such comparisons can provide useful additional information. Such estimates may also be used in the context of estimating compensation for injury, where the person's current position in the distribution is known. In the context of the formation of *expectations* of future earnings (in occupational choice models, or analyses of dynamic or life cycle demand models) this kind of approach can also be useful, as shown in chapter 6 above.

Estimates of lifetime earnings, based on the constant relative position approach, can easily be made using the descriptive model of earnings over life examined in chapter 6. In particular, since earnings in each age group are approximated by the lognormal distribution, there is a simple and convenient relationship between the quantiles of the Normal and the lognormal distributions; see Aitchison and Brown (1957, p. 9). If the qth quantiles of $N(0, 1)$ and $\Lambda(\mu, \sigma^2)$ are denoted v_q and ξ_q respectively, then

$$\xi_q = \exp(\mu + v_q\sigma) \qquad (9.2)$$

and in particular $E(y) = \exp(\mu + \tfrac{1}{2}\sigma^2)$.

Using tables of the standard Normal distribution for the values of v_q, the relationship in (9.2) can therefore be used to provide the profile of any quantile of the distribution over age, given the parameters of the distribution $\Lambda(y_t|\mu_t, \sigma_t^2)$. The profiles of μ_t and σ_t^2 can be estimated following the procedure of chapter 6. In some cases (particularly the discounted value of median earnings, were $v_q = 0$) explicit solutions for the measure of 'lifetime' earnings may be obtained using the method shown in section 6.4 of chapter 6.

Some Empirical Results

Examples of alternative measures of 'lifetime earnings' are shown in table 9.1, for the professions also examined in chapter 6. The term D_i denotes the discounted lifetime earnings of someone earning the ith decile in each year. The basic data were also used by the *Royal Commission on the Distribution of Income and Wealth* (1976, p. 225) to produce diagrams of the profiles of median earnings with age. The age–earnings profiles, based on cross sectional data, have not been adjusted for productivity growth or for the probability of unemployment. Such adjustments would of course need to be made, depending on the context of the analysis.

The inadequacy of a simple comparison of mean lifetime earnings is clearly shown by the table. For example, when comparing solicitors and architects at low interest rates the ranking is different for $E(Y)$ than for D_1 and D_3. Occupational choice would therefore be different for those who expected to be in the lower deciles throughout working life to that for those expecting to be in higher deciles. Similar changes in the ranking also take place when comparing D_1 and D_9 for university teachers with those for engineers, and those for surveyors with those for accountants. At higher rates of interest the orders of magnitude are quite different when comparing different parts of the distribution, although the rankings are consistent. This is, of course, a reflection of the different time profiles of earnings. For general dental practitioners and consultants comparisons of D_1 and D_9 are aso of interest.

9.2 The Dispersion of Lifetime Earnings

The Gibrat Process and the Coefficient of Variation

The coefficient of variation of earnings measured over different time periods, when earnings changes follow Gibrat's Law of Pro-

112   *Time period and distribution of earnings*

Table 9.1   Present values of life earnings at age 23 years: alternative measures (£100s)

Occupation	Rate of interest	D_1	D_3	M	D_7	D_9	$E(Y)$
Surveyors	0.02	197	312	433	604	981	534
	0.06	100	152	204	275	428	242
	0.10	62	90	118	155	232	137
Accountants	0.02	212	314	415	550	829	482
	0.06	106	152	196	253	368	222
	0.10	65	91	114	144	203	127
General dental	0.02	324	496	667	899	1385	786
practitioners	0.06	190	285	378	501	757	438
	0.10	130	193	253	332	492	289
Consultants	0.02	664	872	1053	1273	1675	1125
	0.06	344	443	530	633	819	562
	0.10	216	275	325	385	491	342
University	0.02	291	373	443	526	674	467
teachers	0.06	136	173	204	242	308	215
	0.10	79	99	117	138	175	123
Engineers	0.02	250	341	424	530	735	467
	0.06	132	173	210	255	341	226
	0.10	85	108	128	153	197	136
Solicitors	0.02	256	406	558	768	1221	673
(England and	0.06	118	183	248	336	523	294
Wales)	0.10	67	103	137	184	281	161
Architects	0.02	329	465	591	752	1065	657
	0.06	176	246	310	390	546	342
	0.10	114	157	196	245	339	215

Data from a Report of the *Royal Commission on Doctors' and Dentists' Remuneration* (The Pilkington Commission). Supplement to report. Cmnd 1064.
D_i = life earnings of someone earning the ith decile in each year.
The parameter estimates on which these values are based are given in Creedy (1974, p. 417).

portionate Effect, was examined in chapter 8. The covariance between earnings in different years was shown to take a simple form for substitution into equation (8.3). In the present context it is useful to use Cowell's (1975) correction of Fase's (1971) earlier result, so that the variance of discounted earnings from period t to period T is given by

$$V(Y) = \sum_{s=t}^{T-1} \left(\sum_{r=t}^{s} c_r \bar{y}_r \eta_r^2 + \eta_s^2 \sum_{r=s+1}^{T} c_r \bar{y}_r \right) c_s \bar{y}_s \qquad (9.3)$$

where all terms have been defined earlier. With the substitution of the appropriate profiles of μ_t and σ_t^2 from chapter 6, the profiles of $\bar{y}_t$ and η_t^2 can be obtained using the standard properties of the lognormal distribution.

Some results are shown in table 9.2, which also shows, for comparison, the coefficient of variation in two selected years and the age at which the dispersion of annual earnings is the same as that of discounted lifetime earnings. The latter can easily be calculated given the parameters of the model and the value of $\eta_{(T)}^2$, since the value of t for which $\eta_{(T)}^2$ is equal to η_t^2 is given by

$$t = \{\log(1 + \eta_{(T)}^2) - \eta_0^2\}/\sigma_u^2 \qquad (9.4)$$

It is interesting to note that consultants, with the highest average value of lifetime earnings, have the second lowest coefficient of variation. At higher rates of interest the value of the coefficient of variation of lifetime earnings is nearer that of the lower age group. The last two columns show, for rates of interest of two and ten per cent, the age at which inequality of annual earnings is the same as for lifetime earnings. For low rates of interest this is normally in the late thirties, while for the higher rate of interest this occurs at about 30 years. The extent to which the ranking of occupations by mean lifetime earnings is very different to the ranking according to the coefficient of variation of lifetime earnings may perhaps be regarded as indirect evidence for the existence of non-competing groups in the labour market. The case of consultants is an extreme, but far from isolated, example.

Table 9.2 clearly shows that, while the coefficient of variation of discounted lifetime earnings is lower than that of annual earnings in the higher age groups, it is higher than in the youngest age groups. Chapter 8 showed that it is possible for the measure over a longer period to be lower than in *any* year, and indeed the *Royal Commission on the Distribution of Income and Wealth* suggested that this might in fact be the case. Thus the first report stated 'distributions that show differences between people at every stage of their working life ... are likely to show greater inequality than distributions which record differences between the lifetime

Table 9.2 Dispersion of lifetime earnings: random proportionate changes

Occupation/education	Coefficient of variation (interest rate)			Coefficient of variation of annual earnings		Age at which inequality of annual earnings is same as for lifetime earnings (interest rate)	
	(0.2)	(0.6)	(0.10)	Age 23	Age 62	(0.2)	(0.10)
Surveyors	0.63	0.55	0.49	0.32	0.94	40	31
Accountants	0.52	0.46	0.42	0.30	0.75	39	31
General dental practitioners	0.62	0.54	0.52	0.47	0.78	40	28
Consultants	0.34	0.32	0.31	0.27	0.45	36	30
University teachers	0.32	0.31	0.31	0.29	0.36	36	30
Engineers	0.39	0.34	0.30	0.18	0.61	37	30
Solicitors (England and Wales)	0.63	0.59	0.57	0.50	0.77	40	31
Architects	0.46	0.44	0.42	0.39	0.55	38	28

incomes of the population covered' (1975, p. 147). The result shown in table 9.2 should not however be too surprising in view of the shapes of the profiles of μ_t and σ_t^2.

Serial Correlation in Proportionate Changes

The results of the previous chapter, concerning the covariance between earnings in two years and taken from Fase (1971), can in fact be extended to allow for serial correlation in relative earnings changes. The derivation of the results is rather tedious, but it can be shown that

$$\text{cov}(y_r, y_s) = \bar{y}_r \bar{y}_s \{\exp(\sigma_r^2 + P_{rs}) - 1\} \qquad s > r$$

with

$$P_{rs} = \sigma_\epsilon^2 \sum_{k=1}^{r} \sum_{j=k+1}^{s} \sum_{t=0}^{j} \gamma^{2\tau + j - k} \tag{9.5}$$

Then writing

$$\psi_{rs} = \exp(\sigma_r^2 + P_{rs}) - 1 \tag{9.6}$$

which can be compared with the usual expression for the coefficient of variation of annual earnings of a lognormal distribution, the variance of lifetime earnings $V(Y)$ from t to T is now given by

$$V(Y) = \sum_{s=t}^{T-1} \left(\sum_{r=t}^{s} c_r \bar{y}_r \psi_{rs} + \sum_{r=s+1}^{T} c_r \bar{y}_r \psi_{sr} \right) c_s \bar{y}_s \tag{9.7}$$

Thus in (9.7) ψ_{rs} and ψ_{sr} have been substituted for η_r^2 and η_s^2 respectively in (9.3), except that ψ_{sr} must now be included within the second summation inside the large brackets as it depends on r.

Examination of equation (9.7) for alternative values of γ and σ_ϵ^2 shows however that the coefficient of variation of lifetime earnings is not very sensitive to this assumption. But this result does not allow for serial correlation combined with Galtonian regression, and it is also possible that the measure of dispersion itself may not be very sensitive to the resulting distributional changes. Thus it seems useful to examine lifetime dispersion further, with the use of a simulated population of individuals who follow the various processes of earnings changes.

9.3   A Simulation Analysis

The Simulation Method

The processes of year-to-year earnings changes, described in chapter 4, can easily be adapted for simulation purposes. Consider first the simple Gibrat process, where the basic model is specified by

$$y_{it} = y_{it-1} \exp\{f(t) + u_{it}\} \qquad (9.8)$$

where

$$u_{it} \text{ is } N(0, \sigma_u^2) \qquad (9.9)$$

and

$$y_{i0} \text{ is } \Lambda(\mu_0, \sigma_0^2)$$

and hence

$$x_{i0}(= \log y_{i0}) \text{ is } N(\mu_0, \sigma_0^2) \qquad (9.10)$$

In chapter 6 the profile of μ_t was shown to be quadratic, so

$$\mu_t = \mu_0 + \theta_t - \delta t^2$$

and it was shown that this is consistent with a profile for $f(t)$ that is linear. Then writing, following Brown (1967),

$$f(t) = \alpha(\tau - t) \qquad (9.11)$$

it can be seen that $\alpha = 2\delta$ and $\tau = \theta/2\delta$.

The simulation procedure is as follows. Given a random variable u_{i0}, from a standard Normal distribution, equation (9.10) can be used to obtain the initial earnings x_{i0} of individual i, since $x_{i0} = \mu_0 + \sigma_0 u_{i0}$ and $y_{i0} = \exp(x_{i0})$. By assumption, $(x_{i0} - \mu_0)/\sigma_0$ is distributed as $N(0, 1)$. This can be repeated for any number of individuals to obtain a simulated distribution of initial earnings. For each individual in turn it is then possible to obtain a complete profile of earnings using a large set of random Normal deviates, which can be stored in a matrix $\{v_{it}\}$. Equation (9.9) is used to obtain $u_{it} = \sigma_u v_{it}$, which, along with the appropriate value of $f(t)$ from (9.11), is substituted into (9.8) to generate the subsequent year's earnings. This process yields a complete set of earnings $\{y_{it}\}$.

Where serial correlation in successive relative changes, and Galtonian regression, occur then the generating process becomes

$$y_{it} = \left(\frac{y_{it-1}}{m_{t-1}}\right)^{\beta} \exp(\mu_t + u_{it}) \qquad (9.12)$$

with $m_t = \exp(\mu_t)$ and $u_{it} = \gamma u_{it-1} + \epsilon_{it}$, and

$$\epsilon_{it} \text{ is } N(0, \sigma_\epsilon^2) \qquad (9.13)$$

The initial condition $u_{it} = \epsilon_{it}$ can be used to generate the y_{i0}s, after which (9.12) and (9.13) are used.

Results for Alternative Processes

The simulation approach described above provides a useful basis for a variety of analyses where a life cycle context is required and explicit analytical results cannot be obtained. Subjects include, for example, saving behaviour and wealth accumulation, and comparisons among alternative pension schemes. These are applications where a life cycle approach is necessary, sufficient data do not exist, but the characteristics of age–earnings profiles may be estimated using more limited data.

There is little value in reporting results of various basic simulations which are not part of a wider exercise, but some results may briefly be given here. Suppose that μ_0, σ_0^2, α and τ take values of 7.85, 0.06, 0.003 and 25 respectively. First, the simple case of the Gibrat process, with $\sigma_u^2 = 0.005$, may be considered. Using a simulated 'sample' of 600 individuals, (9.8) to (9.11) were used to generate age–earnings profiles for 45 years. In the sample it is found that μ_t increases to a maximum of 8.681 after 25 years, falling to 8.049 after 45 years. The variance of the logarithms, σ_t^2, increases steadily to 0.264 after 45 years. Taking the discounted value of lifetime earnings of each individual in the sample, using a discount rate of two per cent, gives a distribution of discounted earnings with a variance of logarithms of 0.134. Corresponding values for the coefficient of variation and for 'Atkinson's measure' (with the inequality aversion parameter of 1.6) are 0.344 and 0.091.

Comparisons using different specifications are difficult to make, since they involve different profiles for σ_t^2, but with $\gamma = -0.2$ and $\sigma_\epsilon^2 = 0.008$, σ_t^2 increases to 0.290 after 45 years, and is higher than the previous case in every year. The values of the variance of logarithms, the coefficient of variation and Atkinson's measure, for discounted lifetime earnings (at two per cent), were 0.141, 0.357 and 0.097. The relationship between lifetime inequality and inequality in any particular year is therefore little altered by the negative serial correlation in year-to-year earnings changes. A similar result is obtained when Galtonian regression is assumed, with $\beta = 0.97$, and σ_u^2 raised to 0.02. The value of σ_t^2 is higher in each age group, rising to a maximum of 0.32. But the measures of dispersion of discounted earnings are (in the same order as before) 0.154, 0.381 and 0.105.

Further Reading

This chapter is based on Creedy (1977). The approach has been extended, and applied to the logistic distribution, by Atoda and Tachibanaki (1980). The simulation model has been used in the analysis of state pension schemes in Creedy (1980, 1982a, 1982c). Rather different simulation methods have also been used by Blinder (1974) and Blomquist (1981). An early study of lifetime earnings in the context of human capital analysis, based on cross sectional data, was made by Wilkinson (1966), but a critique of rate of return studies by Merrett (1966) is still worth reading. On much earlier studies of 'the value of man' see the very useful survey by Kiker (1966), while Kiker and Cochrane (1973) concentrate on the 'human costs' of war. Petty's contribution is contained in Hull (1899). For alternative and more recent treatments of lifetime earnings see Moss (1979), Irvine (1981), Friesen and Miller (1983) and Krelle and Shorrocks (1978). The literature relating to the pecuniary value that may be attached to methods of reducing the risk of fatal accidents raises separate issues which are not discussed here.

Part VI

Taxation and Income Redistribution

10

Income Averaging and Progressive Taxation

It is well known that in a progressive tax system higher taxes are paid on fluctuating incomes. In the United Kingdom income is cumulated over the financial year, but only in certain exceptional cases are there any provisions for averaging over a number of years. An obvious implication is that the burden of taxation falls more heavily on individuals with more highly fluctuating incomes, so the question arises of how this burden is distributed over the population. This is complicated to the extent that those with less stable incomes may be compensated by higher absolute incomes, when averaged over a longer period. Furthermore, there may be an incentive for individuals to attempt to achieve a smooth earnings stream, so the difficult question of labour supply is also raised. However, this chapter is concerned with much narrower issues. Section 10.1 examines a simple scheme for income averaging over three years and the consequences for tax liability of changes in income, using a simple hypothetical tax schedule. Section 10.2 then used longitudinal data to examine the implications of this simple schedule for the possible changes in total tax revenue that would result from the adoption of an averaging scheme, and the changes in tax rates required to maintain an unchanged total revenue. Finally a number of issues concerning inequality are briefly examined.

There seems to have been little systematic analysis of the possible effects of income averaging for tax purposes. Considerably more attention has been devoted to the question of the appropriate taxation of 'permanent' and 'temporary' incomes, involving the appropriate concept of income, the classic treatment being that of J. S. Mill (1848). There has, however, been more interest in the United States. Early analyses are by Simons (1938) and by Vickrey (1938), who both favoured some method of averaging. Vickrey suggested that 'the discounted value of the series of tax payments made by any taxpayer should be independent of the way in which his income has been allocated to the various income years' (1938, p. 79). An averaging scheme was introduced in Wisconsin in 1928, but lasted only four years. A further scheme was introduced in 1964, and heavily criticized in David *et al.* (1969). The scheme proposed by Simons (1938, p. 154) was more complex, and allowed for an *ex post* adjustment (after a period of, say, five years) whereby a rebate would be given in cases where the amount that a person would have paid on a constant stream (equal to the average value of the actual income stream) is lower than the amount actually paid by more than ten per cent.

In the United Kingdom the most serious discussions of this subject can be found in the reports of the Royal Commissions of 1920 and 1952, chaired by Colwyn and Radcliffe respectively. In 1920 the Commission suggested that all employees should be taxed on the basis of each year's income, and pointed out that 'the revenue is likely to benefit by the change' (1920, para. 479). At that time weekly wage earners were assessed quarterly, while many salaried people were assessed under schedule D, involving three-year averaging. All employees were moved to schedule E in 1922, however. The possible effect on total revenue will be considered in more detail later in this chapter. The 1952 Commission did not clearly distinguish between income averaging and systems that involve collection in arrears. The latter may provide an interest free loan when income is rising but may involve hardship in the case of an unanticipated fall in income. The system operating in 1940 in the UK, which involved collection in arrears, is discussed in Barr *et al.* (1977, p. 23). Although some averaging schemes have involved collection in arrears, the next section of this chapter considers a scheme that specifically avoids this difficulty.

10.1   A Simple Averaging System

The Assessment of Tax Liability

In order to avoid collection in arrears it is necessary that at the end of each period the total tax liability is met in full by the taxpayer.

Consider the following stages in the assessment of taxation for each individual.

1 In each period calculate the average income over the current and previous two periods. The resulting three-year moving average is denoted $\bar{y}$.
2 Calculate the total tax that would have been paid had income been constant at the value of $\bar{y}$. Thus if the 'nominal' tax schedule involves taxation of $T(y)$ on an income of y, the appropriate figure is simply $3T(\bar{y})$.
3 Calculate the total tax actually paid over the previous two periods. For convenience of exposition at this stage, consider the case where income had been constant in previous years at the value of, say, y. (This assumption is not critical for the following discussion.) The tax paid would then be $2T(y)$.
4 Subtract the value obtained in (iii) from that in (ii). The resulting figure is the tax to be paid in the current period. If income in the third period is y_3, after changing by $100\,\delta$ per cent, the tax to be paid may be denoted $T^*(y_3)$. In the simple case considered here $T^*(y_3) = 3T(\bar{y}) - 2T(y)$.

Changes in Income and the Tax Liability

It is then necessary to consider how the tax liability changes, under a given nominal tax schedule, as a result of a change in income. As above it is assumed that income up to the current period is constant at y, and changes to $y_3 = (1 + \delta)y$ in the current period. However, the opening sentence of this chapter must first be qualified. If a progressive scheme is regarded as one in which the marginal tax rate (MTR) exceeds the average tax rate (ATR), then progression alone is not sufficient to ensure that people with fluctuating incomes pay more tax. In the case of the linear negative income tax, which is progressive but has a constant MTR, it is easy to show that the above system of averaging makes no different to the tax liability. The question of averaging is only relevant where marginal tax rates continually increase with income.

The following analysis is therefore restricted to a simple tax formula which has an increasing MTR. In order to obtain results that can readily be interpreted, it is most convenient to use a simple tractable function which contains only one parameter, k. This single parameter then affects both the 'progressivity, of the system and, combined with the distribution of income, the total tax revenue. The average tax rate $t(y) = T(y)/y$, is given by

$$t(y) = 1 - y^{-k} \qquad k < 1 \tag{10.1}$$

so post-tax income, z, is equal to y^{1-k} and the MTR is $1 - (1-k)y^{-k}$.

This tax formula was suggested by Edgeworth (1925, p. 268) in his discussion of the report of the 1920 Royal Commission, and has often been used since then. Edgeworth also considered the slightly more general form $t(y) = 1 - by^{-k}$ and found that it gave a good fit to a number of actual tax schedules, with b very close to unity. Dalton (1954, p. 68) showed that the above form of equation (10.1) can be derived from the principle of equal proportional sacrifice combined with a logarithmic utility function. This derivation would not however have been supported by Edgeworth, who rejected both proportional sacrifice and the Bernoulli utility function. The choice of this function is necessary in order to focus attention specifically on the effects of averaging, rather than other features of any actual tax system (it does not correspond to the complex UK scheme but is more relevant to other countries).

Using the definitions and assumptions mentioned above, and noting that $\bar{y} = y(3 + \delta)/3$, we have

$$T^*(y_3) = 3[y(3 + \delta)/3 - \{y(3 + \delta)/3\}^{1-k}] - 2(y - y^{1-k})$$

The relevant question here is whether the tax paid in the third period under income averaging is less than the amount that would otherwise be paid where the tax is based on each separate year's income; that is, if $T^*(y_3) < T(y_3)$. In order for this condition to hold it is necessary that

$$3\{(3 + \delta)/3\}^{1-k} > 2 + (1 + \delta)^{1-k} \tag{10.2}$$

Let A and B be the left-hand side and right-hand side respectively of the inequality in (10.2). Now when $\delta = 0$ it can be seen that $A = B$, giving the obvious result that there is no difference in the tax liability. In order to show that the inequality always holds it is therefore only necessary to show that $dA/d\delta > dB/d\delta$ for $\delta > 0$ (that is, for an increase in income of 100 δ per cent), and vice versa for $\delta < 0$. For $\delta > 0$ the required condition is that

$$\{(3 + \delta)/3\}^{-k} > (1 + \delta)^{-k}$$

or

$$\{(3 + 3\delta)/(3 + \delta)\}^k > 1$$

whence

$$1 + 2\delta/(3 + \delta) > 1 \qquad\qquad (10.3)$$

and this inequality always holds. The same steps also confirm that when $\delta < 0$, $dA/d\delta < dB/d\delta$. The individual is therefore better off in an averaging system when income falls than he would be in a system without averaging. Furthermore, it is clear that this is without prejudice to any future tax liability. The explanation of this result is of course straightforward, since under the averaging system some of the tax that would otherwise have to be paid in the current year has been pre-paid in the previous two years, but with no extra burden imposed in those years. Conversely, when income rises the tax liability for the current year is actually less than would otherwise be the case, because $\bar{y}$ is reduced by the lower incomes of previous years. The property of increasing MTR guarantees that the reduction for this reason more than compensates for the fact that $\bar{y}$ exceeds the average of the earlier two years. Thus, insofar as incentives are affected by high marginal tax rates, they would be expected to be higher in a system that is based on income averaging.

Further analysis of averaging clearly requires either a well specified model of individual relative income mobility, or longitudinal data covering a number of consecutive periods. However, with even a simple model of mobility the analysis soon becomes intractable, so the next section uses longitudinal data.

10.2   Further Analysis Using Longitudinal Data

This section uses information provided by the Department of Health and Social Security (UK) about the earnings of three cohorts of males over the three-year period 1971–2–3. The cohorts were born in 1923, 1933 and 1943, and the samples are the same as those used in chapter 8 above. It is important to note that these data are used for illustrative purposes, since no information is avilable about the family circumstances and allowances claimed by each individual, and of course a hypothetical tax function is used. They do however accurately reflect earnings mobility, and from the point of view of the present chapter this is the most critical element in the analysis. So long as the conditions that affect allowances change slowly relative to earnings changes, the results should still be of interest.

Changes in Total Revenue

The total tax revenue per person is simply the difference between average pre-tax and average post-tax income. The analysis is therefore considerably simplified if a convenient transformation exists between the two distributions of y and z. Such a transformation exists for the tax schedule used in section 10.1 and the case where incomes are lognormally distributed. Thus if the distribution function, $F(x)$, is $\Lambda(\mu, \sigma^2)$, where μ and σ^2 are the mean and variance respectively of the logarithms of income, then it can be shown, using Aitchison and Brown (1957, p. 11, theorem 2.3), that

$$z = y^{1-k} \text{ is } \Lambda(\mu(1-k), (1-k)^2 \sigma^2) \tag{10.4}$$

Using this result, the means of y and z, $\bar{y}$ and $\bar{z}$ respectively, are given by

$$\bar{y} = \exp(\mu + \tfrac{1}{2}\sigma^2)$$

and $\hfill (10.5)$

$$\bar{z} = \exp\{\mu(1-k) + \tfrac{1}{2}(1-k)^2 \sigma^2\}$$

Equation (10.5) can be used to obtain the tax per person when each year's income is taxed separately, given the annual values of μ and σ^2. The problem remains of obtaining the corresponding values for the distribution of average income over three years. This problem has been discussed extensively in Part V of this book, but for present purposes it is assumed that the distribution of the sum of income over three years can also be approximated by the lognormal distribution. Thus if the sum, Y, is distributed as $\Lambda(M, V^2)$, average income, $Y/3$, is distributed as $\Lambda(M - \log 3, V^2)$. Under an averaging system the distribution of post-tax income can be obtained using (10.4) so average post-tax income, $\bar{z}^*$ say, is given by

$$\bar{z}^* = \exp\{(1-k)(M - \log 3) + \tfrac{1}{2}(1-k)^2 \sigma^2\} \tag{10.6}$$

The values of μ and σ^2 for each year, and M and V^2 for each cohort are given in table 10.1. These are used to obtain table 10.2, which shows the tax paid for various periods for two values of k.

For cohort 1943 it can be seen that a conventional progressive tax system with $k = 0.05$ would raise £1925 ($= 537 + 647 + 741$) per person over the three years, whereas the alternative averaging system would raise £1860 ($= 3$ times 620). In each case the average tax rate works out at approximately 32%, but the fall in total

Table 10.1 Summary measures of alternative distributions

	Tax year			Sum of three years
	1971	1972	1973	
Cohort 1943				
Geometric mean	1516	1776	2010	5443
Variance of logs	0.240	0.256	0.254	0.146
Cohort 1933				
Geometric mean	1707	2024	2223	6078
Variance of logs	0.303	0.203	0.243	0.170
Cohort 1923				
Geometric mean	1645	1850	2082	5680
Variance of logs	0.247	0.259	0.222	0.174

Table 10.2 Total tax revenue over three years

Time period	$\bar{y}$	$\bar{z}$		$\bar{y} - \bar{z}$	
		$k = 0.05$	$k = 0.10$	$k = 0.05$	$k = 0.10$
Cohort 1943					
1971	1709	1172	803	537	906
1972	2018	1371	932	647	1026
1973	2282	1541	1041	741	1241
(1971 + 1972 + 1973)/3	1951	1331	909	620	1042
Cohort 1933					
1971	1986	1349	917	637	1069
1972	2240	1516	1026	724	1214
1973	2510	1687	1135	823	1375
(1971 + 1972 + 1973)/3	2205	1495	1013	711	1191
Cohort 1923					
1971	1861	1270	867	591	994
1972	2016	1427	968	673	1137
1973	2326	1570	1061	756	1265
(1971 + 1972 + 1973)/3	2965	1404	955	661	1110

Note: $\bar{y}$ is obtained using $\exp(\mu + \frac{1}{2}\sigma^2)$, rather than the actual value of the arithmetic mean. Thus the lognormal assumption is consistently used throughout the calculations. All calculations were made before the figures were rounded to the nearest pound.

revenue as a consequence of 'changing' to an averaging scheme is of the order of 3.4%. For the more progressive system with $k = 0.10$, implying an overall tax rate of about 53%, the fall in total revenue is of a similar order of magnitude; that is, 3.3%. Similarly for cohort 1933 the reduction in total revenue would be 2.3% for both values of k; while for chort 1923 the reduction would be 2.1% with $k = 0.05$, falling to 1.9% for $k = 0.10$. The fact that the percentage revenue loss that would result from a change in the system is lower for the higher age groups is an expected consequence of the slightly higher earnings mobility within the younger cohort, whose members experience more short term unemployment. It is perhaps worth noting that these results may 'overstate' the revenue loss if averaging does have a significant effect on labour supply.

Equal Revenue Taxes

The previous section considered the revenue loss that would result from a change to an averaging system of taxation, with the tax schedule unchanged. It is also of interest to examine the required change in the tax schedule (in this case, the parameter k) that would be required to maintain a constant total revenue.

Equation (10.6) gives the average post-tax income where tax is assessed on the average of three years' income, and equation (10.5) gives the average post-tax income where tax is based on each year independently. Each is a function of the value of k, and they may be written as $\bar{z}^*(k)$, and $\bar{z}_i(k)$ for the ith year. For total revenue to remain unchanged it is required to choose a value of k, k' say, such that

$$\bar{z}^*(k') = \frac{1}{3} \sum_{i=1}^{3} \bar{z}_i(k) \qquad (10.7)$$

The value of the right-hand side of (10.7), and therefore the required value of $\bar{z}^*(k')$, can be obtained from the values given in table 10.2. For example, consider cohort 1933 with $k = 0.05$, where it is equal to £1517 (average of 1347, 1516 and 1687). The value of k' may then be obtained by using the appropriate values of M and V^2 from table 10.1 and solving the quadratic equation in (10.6). In this example it is found that in order to ensure a constant value of £1517 for $\bar{z}^*$, the parameter of the tax function should be raised to $k' = 0.058$. This result may be used to calculate the difference in the annual tax that has to be paid by an individual with a constant income, as a result of a change to an averaging system that maintains total revenue at its former level. For someone with a constant income of, for example, £1400 per year, the difference is £55 per year; while an individual with a constant income of £2500 per year would pay additional taxes of £103 per year. This difference increases to £170 when pre-tax income is constant at £4000.

Inequality of Post-tax Incomes

It has already been mentioned that equity issues are raised insofar as more highly fluctuating earnings are not compensated by relatively higher average earnings. If this kind of compensation does occur, then a change to averaging would obviously shift the burden of taxation towards the relatively lower paid, and would increase the inequality of post-tax earnings measured over a three-year period. Longitudinal data are therefore very useful here, and a direct approach (rather than considering mobility separately) involves a comparison of a measure of the inequality of post-tax earnings over three years, under the two different systems. Measures of discounted earnings were also considered, but the period is too short for discounting to have a significant effect.

Thus, with the individual data it is possible to calculate the sum of post-tax earnings over three years when each year is taxed independently; that is Σy_i^{1-k}. The distribution of post-tax earnings when tax is based on the three-year average can be obtained directly from the values of M and V^2 in table 10.1, using the transformation in equation (10.4). However, the calculations reveal little difference between the two sets of measures.

These results therefore suggest that there is very little variation in relative mobility over the range of income distribution observed here, and that there would not be expected to be any systematic effect on inequality resulting from the introduction of an averaging system. If may, however, be suggested that the comparison should not use the same value of k for both types of system, but should be between schemes that raise the same total revenue. For cohort 1933 with $k = 0.05$ it was noted that with averaging k would have to be raised to 0.058 for constant revenue. This would give a value of 0.151 for the variance of logarithms of post-tax earnings over three years, implying a slightly larger reduction than shown in table 10.3.

Table 10.3 Inequality of post-tax incomes over three years (variance of logarithms)

	Cohort 1943		Cohort 1933		Cohort 1923	
Tax period	$k = 0.05$	$k = 0.10$	$k = 0.05$	$k = 0.10$	$k = 0.05$	$k = 0.10$
1 year	0.133	0.120	0.154	0.139	0.158	0.142
3 years	0.132	0.118	0.153	0.138	0.157	0.141

Further Reading

This chapter is based on Creedy (1979a). For a further example of the use of the simple tax function see Atkinson (1983). The averaging systems used previously in the UK are described in Barr *et al.* (1977). A selection of detailed studies of specific averaging provisions is Tibbetts (1940), Steger (1956), Merkies (1968), Chisholm (1971) and Kesselman (1982). For a useful discussion of progressive taxation in a lifetime perspective with imperfect capital markets, see Polinsky (1974). It is well known that with an accretion concept of income, a problem arises over the treatment of capital gains since they can only realistically be taxed when they are realized. The use of income averaging has therefore also been suggested in this context.

11

Some Analytics of Income Tax and Transfer Systems

Although there has been a great deal of discussion of the relative merits of alternative income maintenance schemes, the precise relationships between benefit levels and tax rates required are not usually examined in detail. Where specific schemes have been proposed (as for example in Meade *et al.*, 1978) the costs have usually been estimated for specified levels of benefits, but the more general nature of the policy choices involved have not been examined. The purpose of the present chapter is to provide comparable results for a number of simple income tax and transfer schemes, so that the trade-offs involved in policy decisions can easily be examined and compared.

The starting point of the following analysis is the idea of the budget constraint; that within any type of scheme the revenue raised by taxation must be sufficient to finance the benefits paid to specified groups. The existence of the budget constraint means that a degree of freedom is lost in setting a number of policy variables, such as tax and benefit rates and income thresholds. This makes it useful to express the tax rate required in any scheme in terms of the other policy variables, and the distribution of pre-tax-and-transfer income. In the following sections the considerable complications raised by labour supply responses and differences in family size and composition will be ignored, in order to focus attention on the basic nature of the schemes. Section 11.1 considers some very basic negative income tax and other transfer schemes, and section 11.2 then adds social insurance contributions to income tax in order to finance the transfer payments. When discussing the 'redistributive' effect of such schemes, most earlier analyses concentrate on the total value of income transfers among broad groups. However, section 11.3 provides a method of calculating a measure of the dispersion of post-tax-and-transfer income, based on the various transformations involved. Finally, section 11.4 briefly gives some numerical examples, based on explicit assumptions about the distribution of pre-tax-and-transfer income.

11.1   The Basic Schemes

The Negative Income Tax and Social Dividend

The distinction between the negative income tax (NIT) and social dividend (SD) schemes is administrative, since they both involve the same relationship beween pre- and post-transfer income. This is shown in figure 11.1 where y and z denote pre- and post-transfer income respectively. With no transfers the relationship between z and y is the 45° line OF. Under the social dividend scheme an unconditional payment equal to OT is paid to each person, and all other income is taxed at a constant poportional rate, t, resulting in the line TT. Under NIT the tax function is written as $T(y) = t(y - a)$,

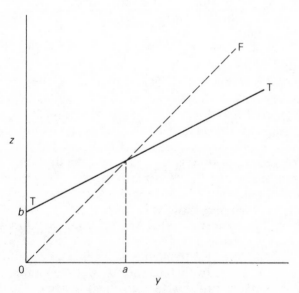

Figure 11.1   Negative income tax and social dividend.

and negative values of $T(y)$ are actually paid to the individual. The two schemes can be expressed as follows:

fot NIT: $\quad z = y - T(y) = y - t(y - a) = y(1 - t) + at$

$$(11.1)$$

for SD: $\quad z = b + y - T(y) = b + y - ty = y(1 - t) + b$

$$(11.2)$$

These are equivalent when $b = at$. The slope of the line TT is therefore $(1 - t)$. Each scheme requires two policy variables to be set, but there is only one degree of freedom since the net tax revenue must be sufficient to finance the payment of the social dividend. When the distribution function of income is $F(y)$, then it is required for the NIT scheme that

$$\int t(y - a) \, dF(y) = 0 \qquad (11.3)$$

Equation (11.3) shows that $a = \bar{y}$, the arithmetic mean income, whatever the tax rate, t. Thus there is net redistribution from those above to those below the arithmetic mean; the extent of the redistribution is determined by the tax rate. It is useful to express t in terms of the basic minimum, b:

$$t = b/\bar{y} \qquad (11.4)$$

This type of scheme therefore involves a fairly large amount of redistribution. Because of the linearity of the schedule over the whole range of income, the redistribution can be easily expressed in terms of the coefficients of variation of pre- and post-transfer income, η_y and η_z respectively. It can be shown that

$$\eta_z = \eta_y \{ 1 + b/(1 - t) \, \bar{y} \}^{-1} \qquad (11.5)$$

Non-linear transformations are examined in section 11.3 below. In practice, income taxation is used to raise more revenue than is required to finance a transfer system; that is, net revenue must exceed zero. Suppose that it is required to raise an amount of net revenue equal to r per person, using income taxation. The above result in equation (11.4) may then be modified, such that $t = (b + r)/\bar{y}$. In the following results it is only necessary to write $b + r$ instead of b. However, a major problem with these schemes is that because of their 'generosity' to those below arithmetic mean earnings the NIT/SD schemes must either involve a very high marginal tax rate, or a very low basic minimum b.

A minimum income guarantee

The most basic form of minimum income guarantee (MIG) involves raising the incomes, of all those with gross incomes below a specified level, to a guaranteed minimum. However, MIG presents several possibilities. Consider figure 11.2, where the relationship between z and y for a simple tax structure, using a single tax rate, t, and allowances of a, is shown as 0CT. Thus individuals pay no tax on earnings below a, and pay a constant proportion of earnings measured above a:

$$T(y) = 0 \qquad y \leqslant a$$
$$= t(y - a) \qquad y > a$$

The simplest form of MIG would involve the payment of $(a - y)$ to all those with $y < a$. This would produce a relationship between z and y of BCT. It is clear that this would involve the payment of higher transfers to a smaller number of people than under the

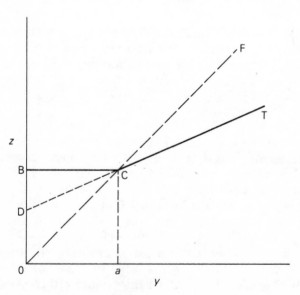

Figure 11.2   Minimum income guarantee.

NIT/SD scheme, for any given tax rate. For zero net revenue it is required that payments are equal to receipts; that is

$$\int^a (a - y)\,dF(y) = t\int_a (y - a)\,dF(y) \tag{11.6}$$

This can be simplified using the concept of the moment distribution. The rth incomplete moment distribution $F_r(y)$ is defined as

$$F_r(y) = \int^y u^r\,dF(u)\bigg/\int u^r\,dF(u) \tag{11.7}$$

where the denominator of (11.7) is the rth moment of y about the origin, μ_r'. Using (11.7) it can be seen that in general

$$\int_a y^r\,dF(y) = \mu_r'\{1 - F_r(a)\} \tag{11.8}$$

For $r = 1$, then $\mu_1' = \bar{y}$, and the relationship between $F(y)$ and $F_1(y)$ defines the well known Lorenz curve. In the present context it is useful to define the term $G(a)$ using

$$G(a) = \{1 - F_1(a)\} - (a/\bar{y})\{1 - F(a)\} \tag{11.9}$$

Equation (11.6) can then be simplified, using (11.8) and (11.9) to give the tax rate t required to support any specified value of a. Thus after some manipulation it can be shown that

$$t = 1 - (1 - a/\bar{y})/G(a) \tag{11.10}$$

In (11.10) the tax rate is expressed simply in terms of the value of the MIG, which is equal to the level of tax allowances. This system can however be administered in several different ways. It may use a conventional tax system for those with $y > a$, and means-testing may be used to bring those below a up to the level of MIG. Alternatively it may use a combination of either NIT or SD (which produces the schedule 0DT), with means-testing to raise the segment DC to BC.

It is not of course necessary to have the kink, in the schedule relating z and y, at the point C. It would be possible to extend the range of income, over which the effective marginal rate of tax is 100 per cent, to the right of a. Alternatively a MIG scheme may be devised in which fewer individuals receive more generous support.

In either case two policy instruments, the earnings level below which individuals receive MIG, y_0, and the level of MIG itself, b, must be set. But it is important to stress that only one of these can be set independently for given values of a and t. The two alternatives are shown in figure 11.3. In (a), individuals between a and y_0

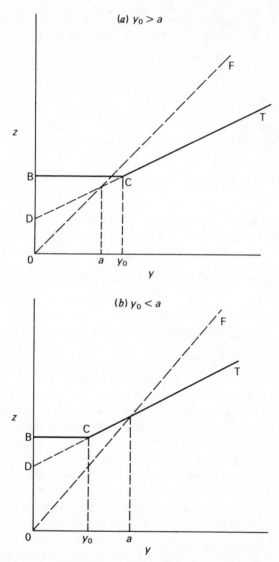

Figure 11.3   Alternative forms of minimum income guarantee.

pay tax *and* receive benefits, with the combined effect giving a 100 per cent 'effective' marginal tax rate. In (*b*), those between y_0 and *a* pay no tax and although they receive smaller absolute transfers than those below y_0, they are not subject to the 100 per cent effective rate.

In each case in figure 11.3 the necessity to ensure continuity at point C provides a relationship between y_0, *b*, *a* and *t*. From the equation of DT it is clear that

$$b = at + (1-t)y_0 \tag{11.11}$$

However, it is usually more convenient to allow *t*, *b* and y_0 to determine *a*, since *b* and y_0 are the policy variables of more direct interest. In this case

$$a = y_0 + (b-y_0)/t \tag{11.12}$$

It is then necessary to consider the condition required for the net tax revenue to be zero; for net revenue to be just sufficient to finance net transfers. In either of the above cases it can be seen that the *net* tax paid by those with *y* below y_0 is $y-b$; and the *net* tax paid by those above y_0 is $ty + y_0(1-t) - b$. The condition is therefore

$$0 = \int^{y_0} (y-b)\,dF(y) + \int_{y_0} \{ty + y_0(1-t) - b\}\,dF(y) \tag{11.13}$$

After some manipulation, using the expressions (11.8) and (11.9), this can be simplified to give

$$t = 1 - (1 - b/\bar{y})/G(y_0) \tag{11.14}$$

which may be compared with equation (11.10). After obtaining the value of *t* for any given *b* and y_0 from (11.14), substitution into (11.12) gives the appropriate value of *a*. Here it is important to stress that only combinations that give positive values of *a* are sensible; otherwise the income tax system involves lump sum tax payments rather than 'allowances', thereby making the system regressive.

The introduction of a higher marginal rate, t_2, applied to incomes above, say, a_2, can also be examined using this framework. The analysis proceeds by writing the net tax paid for individuals in each of the three sections; for $y < y_0$; for $y_0 < y < a_2$; and for $y > a_2$. The condition that total net tax paid is zero can then be used to express t in terms of a_2, t_2, y_0 and b. After some tedious manipulation, this can be shown to give the result that

$$t = \{G(y_0) + t_2 G(a_2) - (1 - b/\bar{y})\}/\{G(y_0) + G(a_2)\} \qquad (11.15)$$

It can be seen that the substitution of $t_2 = t$ into (11.15) produces equation (11.14).

The Modified Minimum Income Guarantee

Each of the minimum income guarantee schemes considered above involves effective marginal rates of 100 per cent below a given income, and it has therefore been suggested that incentives are reduced. An alternative scheme may be devised in which the section BC of the relationship between z and y has a slope of $1 - s$, so that the effective rate is equal to s.

For those below y_0 the net tax paid, $(y - z)$, is $sy - b$; while for those above y_0, gross income, z, is $b + y_0(1-s) + (1-t)(y-y_0)$. Thus net tax is $ty + y_0(s - t) - b$. If the procedure used above is again applied to ensure that the *total* net tax paid is zero, the following relationship is obtained:

$$t = s - (s - b/\bar{y})/G(y_0) \qquad (11.16)$$

and not surprisingly the substitution of $s = 1$ into equation (11.16) gives (11.14).

11.2   National Insurance Contributions

In most countries income taxation is not the only form of direct taxation that is related to income from employment. An additional tax is levied in the form of some type of 'social insurance' contribution, although of course the benefits are not related to past contributions as they would be in an insurance scheme. There are usually differences between the two tax systems, concerning for example the appropriate time period of assessment and the definition of the tax base. Complications are also raised by the existence of employers' contributions, expressed as a proportion of the employee's gross earnings, and by the ability of some people to contract out of certain parts of government social insurance.

The following analysis abstracts from most of these complications, and concentrates on the implications of basing social insurance contributions on gross earnings (rather than a measure of taxable income), and of using an upper earnings limit. For convenience all income is assumed to arise from employment. In Britain National Insurance contributions (NI) are paid on gross earnings up to a maximum, and are not paid until earnings exceed a lower limit. The marginal contributions rate is therefore very high at the lower limit, and is zero above the upper limit. If the upper earnings limit is denoted y_U, and if the value of y_0 (below which individuals have their gross earnings brought up to b) is above the lower earnings limit above which NI is paid, there are again three linear segments to the schedule relating z to y. With NI the marginal effective rate on higher incomes is *lower* than that applying to incomes between y_0 and y_U. The case of MIG with NI (and single tax rate, t) can be examined using the procedure described above. It is worth noting that, because NI is proportional to gross earnings, care must be taken in setting the appropriate level of 'allowances' for the income tax schedule. Following the usual procedure it is then possible to relate the tax rate, t, to the other parameters (or policy variables) of the system, for zero (or some specified amount of) net revenue. Thus

$$t = 1 - (1 - b/\bar{y})/G(y_0) - c\,\{1 - G(y_U)/G(y_0)\} \qquad (11.17)$$

The last term on the right-hand side of (11.17) therefore indicates the extent to which the required tax rate may be reduced with the introduction of NI. However, it can be seen that this last term can never exceed the value of c, so if NI contributions were eliminated the tax rate would not be reduced by the full amount of the NI rate, if the other parameters of the system remain constant. Similarly when the other parameters are held constant an increase in c means that the amount required to finance transfers to those below y_0 would be increased. Thus the tax rate could not be reduced by the same amount as the increase in c.

Total Revenue from Income Tax and National Insurance
It is of interest to consider only the revenue aspects of combining income taxation with NI contributions, ignoring the way in which some of the revenue may be redistributed to specified low income groups. Under the simple income tax schedule used above, with a constant marginal rate applied to earnings measured above a level of allowances, the total revenue per person, R_t, is given by

$$R_t = \int T(y)\,\mathrm{d}F(y)$$

Using the concept of moment distributions, and the simplifications given in equations (11.8) and (11.9), this can be shown to give

$$R_t = t\bar{y}G(a) \tag{11.18}$$

Since $G(0) = 1$, a proportional tax on gross earnings would give a value of revenue per person of simply $t\bar{y}$. Now if the lower earnings limit for NI contributions is denoted y_L (note that in the earlier treatment it was implicitly assumed that $y_L < a < y_0$, which is in fact the case in Britain), the total value of contributions per person, R_c, is given by

$$R_c = c\bar{y}\{1 - F_1(y_L) - G(y_U)\} \tag{11.19}$$

Equations (11.18) and (11.19) can then be used to examine the combination of changes in c and t that leave total revenue per person, $R = R_c + R_t$, unchanged. Setting the total derivative of R equal to zero gives the result that

$$dt/dc = -\{1 - F_1(y_L) - G(y_U)/G(a)\} \tag{11.20}$$

Although it has often been suggested that the two systems of direct taxation should be integrated, the full implications have received surprisingly little attention. It is usually assumed that for unchanged total revenue the tax rate would simply be increased by the value of the NI contributions rate. But since the numerator exceeds the denominator in (11.20), it can be seen that an *increase* in the contributions rate of one percentage point can be accompanied by a *decrease* in the marginal tax rate of more than one percentage point. The simple addition of the two rates gives a misleading impression about the 'overall' rate. Where these implications are not generally appreciated, there is a clear incentive for governments to increase revenue by raising the NI contributions rate rather than by raising the standard rate of income tax. This is precisely what has happened in Britain in recent years.

11.3   The Dispersion of Post-transfer Income

The analysis of the redistributive effects of taxes and transfers involves a number of well known difficulties, associated for example with tax incidence and labour supply. There are in addition the conceptual problems that have led some critics to describe the whole exercise as chimerical. These important issues cannot however be discussed here, and the limited purpose of the present section is to provide a convenient method of calculating a measure of the dispersion of post-tax-and-transfer income where the tax system can be described in terms of a number of linear transformations of pre-tax-and-transfer income.

The relationship between the coefficient of variation of post-transfer and pre-transfer income, η_z and η_y respectively, was given in equation (11.5) for the case of the NIT/SD scheme. This was simplified by the fact that the same linear transformation between z and y applied to the complete distribution. In the other cases examined above it is necessary to decompose the population into a number of separate groups. For example in the case of the simple or modified MIG schemes there are two groups to be considered, those below and above y_0. Analytical results can therefore only be obtained where the measure of dispersion used can also be decomposed in a convenient way. In general there are 'within' and 'between' group effects on overall dispersion. This section presents a general method of calculating the coefficient of variation of z for any number of groups.

Suppose that in the ith group, which covers pre-transfer incomes between y_i and y_j ($y_j > y_i$), the transformation between z and y is given by

$$z = \alpha_i + \beta_i y \qquad (11.21)$$

Define the mean and variance of pre-transfer income *within* the ith group as $\bar{y}_i$ and s_{yi}^2 respectively; then from (11.21) the mean and variance of post-transfer income within the ith group, $\bar{z}_i$ and s_{zi}^2 respectively, are

$$\bar{z}_i = \alpha_i + \beta_i \bar{y}_i \qquad (11.22)$$

$$s_{zi}^2 = \beta_i^2 s_{yi}^2 \qquad (11.23)$$

If w_i is the proportion of individuals in the ith group, then the overall mean and variance of z, $\bar{z}$ and s_z^2, are

$$\bar{z} = \Sigma w_i \bar{z}_i \qquad (11.24)$$

$$s_z^2 = \Sigma w_i (s_{zi}^2 + \bar{z}_i^2) - \bar{z}^2 \qquad (11.25)$$

whence

$$\eta_z = s_z / \bar{z} \qquad (11.26)$$

It is then only necessary to obtain expressions for the w_is and $\bar{y}_i$s and s_{yi}^2s for substitution into (11.24) to (11.26). If $\bar{y}$ and s_y^2 are the mean and variance of y, then it can be seen that

$$w_i = F(y_j) - F(y_i) \tag{11.27}$$

$$\bar{y}_i = \bar{y}\{F_1(y_j) - F_1(y_i)\}/w_i \tag{11.28}$$

$$s_{yi}^2 = (\bar{y} + s_y^2)\{F_2(y_j) - F_2(y_i)\}/w_i - \bar{y}_i^2 \tag{11.29}$$

In (11.29), $F_2(y)$ is the incomplete second moment distribution of y. For the highest income group $F(y_j) = F_1(y_j) = F_2(y_j) = 1$, while for the lowest group $F(y_i) = F_1(y_i) = F_2(y_i) = 0$. The analysis of the redistributive effects of alternative schemes, in terms of the dispersion of the distributions, is obviously much more cumbersome than the analysis of the relationship between tax rates and benefit levels. In practice, however, the above method can be readily used in a wide variety of situations.

11.4   Some Numerical Examples

All of the results obtained in the previous three sections of this chapter are completely general, and do not depend on the form of the distribution of pre-tax-and-transfer income. In particular, it is clear that in every system considered the relationship between the required tax rate and the basic minimum post-transfer income is linear. In some cases, notably equations (11.4), (11.16) and (11.17), the slope of each relationship is the same; only the absolute value of t differs between schemes. Precise values, for comparing alternative combinations, can however only be obtained after making explicit assumptions about the precise form of the distribution function $F(y)$. The use of the lognormal distribution for this purpose is therefore discussed first.

The Lognormal Moment Distribution Functions

Calculations, using the analytical results presented above, can most conveniently be carried out on the assumption that the distribution of pre-tax-and-transfer income is lognormal; so $F(y)$ is $\Lambda(y|\mu, \sigma^2)$. This is because there is a very simple relationship among the moment distribution functions of the lognormal. Aitchison and Brown (1957, p. 12, theorem 2.6) show that the jth moment distribution, denoted $\Lambda_j(y|\mu, \sigma^2)$ is given by

$$\Lambda_j(y|\mu, \sigma^2) = \Lambda(y|\mu + j\sigma^2, \sigma^2) \tag{11.30}$$

Since log *y* is Normally distributed, calculations may be performed using either a table of the standard Normal distribution $N(0, 1)$, or a standard polynomial approximation, such as that given in Aitchison and Brown (1957, p. 71). Some general idea of the form of the distribution functions, and of the very useful function $G(y)$, is shown in figure 11.4. The curves are drawn for a lognormal distribution with arithmetic mean income and coefficient of variation of income respectively of £6000 and 0.5, so that the mean and variance of the logarithms are 8.5879 and 0.2231 respectively.

Minimum Income Guarantee with NI Contributions

The characteristics of the minimum income guarantee, financed by income taxation and National Insurance contributions, are illustrated in figure 11.5. The distribution of *y* used in the calculations is the same as that shown in figure 11.4. Employers' NI contributions have been ignored, and it is assumed that all direct taxes are borne fully by employees. The left-hand side of figure 11.5 shows the relationship between the income tax rate and NI

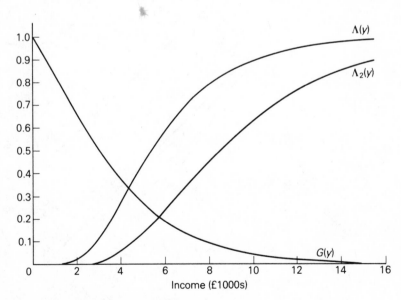

Figure 11.4 Characteristics of the Λ distribution.

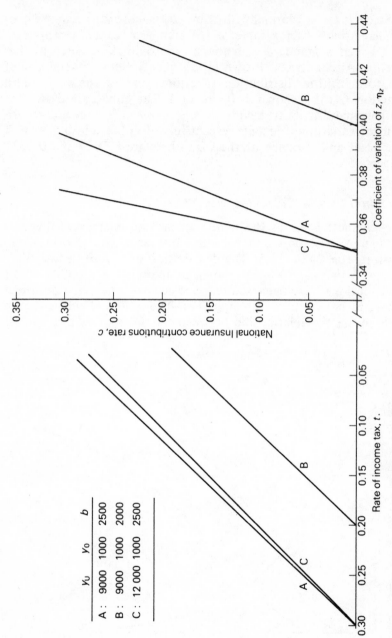

Figure 11.5 A tax/transfer system with NI contributions.

contributions rate required to finance a system with given values of y_U, y_0 and b. These lines are obtained using equation (11.17) above. It is clear that a change in the minimum net income, b, for those with $y < y_0$, has a significant effect on the relationship, as can be seen by a comparison of schedules A and B. However, a change in the upper earnings limit y_U has very little effect.

The effect on the dispersion of net income can then be found using the approach described in section 11.3. In this example the population needs only to be divided into three separate groups (since it is assumed that $y_0 > a > y_L$, as in the British system). The transformations between z and y for the various ranges are

$$z = b \qquad\qquad\qquad\qquad\qquad\qquad y < y_0$$

$$z = b + (y - y_0)(1 - c - t) \qquad\qquad\quad y_0 \leqslant y \leqslant y_U$$

$$z = b + (y_U - y_0)(1 - c - t) + (1 - t)(y - y_U) \quad y > y_U$$

The results are illustrated on the right-hand side of figure 11.5, where it can be seen that the relationship between c and η_z is linear in each case, although this is not obvious from the formulae. The 'regressive' effect of National Insurance contributions can clearly be seen from the figure. The upper earnings limit has relatively little effect from the point of view of revenue raising, but has a much larger effect on the dispersion of incomes. It is therefore suggested that an analysis of this kind can usefully provide an indication of the nature of those 'trade-offs' that must inevitably be made among different policy objectives. In such an interdependent tax system the precise effects of alternative policies are far from transparent.

Further Reading

This chapter is based largely on Creedy (1982b). The detailed results for the implications of National Insurance contributions are taken from Creedy (1981, 1982). Further analysis of alternative negative income tax schemes can be found in Creedy (1978a), and in Creedy and Disney (1985). The basic approach can also be used to examine alternative pension schemes in a two-period model, as in Creedy (1980a, 1982c). A useful discussion of the use of moment distributions in economics is in Hart (1975).

12

The Built-in Flexibility of Income Tax

Previous chapters have concentrated on the nature and implications of relative earnings changes of individuals, but the present chapter abstracts from such changes and examines the effect of a general increase in incomes over time. It is well known that if personal allowances are not indexed to allow for inflation, then a general increase in money incomes will increase tax revenue per person for two reasons. First, it increases taxable income as a proportion of total income for those already paying income tax, and secondly it brings more people into the tax 'net'. The precise extent of this built-in flexibility depends on the way in which marginal tax rates increase as income increases, and on the distribution of before-tax income.

A variety of methods has been used to examine the built-in flexibility of the UK tax system. A survey was provided by Dorrington (1974) who presented a comprehensive simulation analysis. Hutton and Lambert (1980) suggested a method of calculating revenue elasticities for a system consisting of a sequence of fixed marginal tax rates and thresholds. Hutton and Lambert (1980a) also proposed a model of the UK tax system which they described as a 'linear Pareto' model, since it has a fixed marginal rate applying to a large proportion of taxable income and a structure of higher marginal rates applying to top incomes which are assumed to follow the Pareto distribution.

While previous studies have usually estimated the built-in flexibility of a particular tax structure for specific years, the present chapter presents a model that is capable of identifying some of the general properties of a progressive income tax system. The model can be used to provide schedules of total revenue, effective marginal rates and revenue elasticities as income increases. This allows the effects of discretionary changes in the tax system at different average income levels to be isolated. A simple, but extremely flexible, tax function is used which is capable of reproducing the essential features of many progressive tax systems in use. A non-linear tax schedule is used in conjunction with a lognormal distribution of pre-tax incomes, which has the advantage of covering the complete range of income. Thus the model may be described as a 'non-linear lognormal' model. In addition to being very flexible, it has the advantages of tractability, and of being able to capture the main characteristics of actual systems with few parameters. These properties are particularly important where the model is to be integrated into a wider fiscal analysis. Before examining the properties of alternative systems in section 12.2, the main details of the model are described in section 12.1

12.1   A Simple Tax Model

The Tax Schedule

Consider the following income tax schedule, which uses a single value of 'personal' allowances applied to every individual. As in chapter 11, this simplifying assumption is not entirely realistic for most income tax systems, but it is not difficult to obtain a representative value. A single value of allowances was also used by Hutton and Lambert in their 'linear Pareto' model. Denoting total tax as $T(y)$ we have, in the absence of a negative income tax,

$$
\begin{aligned}
T(y) &= 0 & y &< a_1 \\
&= t_1(y - a_1) & a_1 &\leqslant y \leqslant a_2 \\
&= t_1(a_2 - a_1) + (c - hy^{-k})(y - a_2) & y &> a_2
\end{aligned} \tag{12.1}
$$

with

$$h = (c - t_1)a_2^k \tag{12.2}$$

$$k < 1 \tag{12.3}$$

A 'standard rate', t_1, is therefore applied to incomes between the thresholds a_1 and a_2. Thereafter marginal rates increase non-linearly. This schedule can also be applied to tax systems that do not use a standard rate, by setting t_1 and a_1 to zero. Equation (12.2) must then be respecified as $h = (c - m)a_2^k$, where m is the marginal tax rate at the level of income, a_2, at which individuals begin to pay tax. Without a standard rate the function is therefore described by only four parameters, c, m, a_2 and k. The condition in (12.2) ensures that the marginal tax rate at the level, a_2, beyond which individuals pay higher marginal rates of income tax, is equal to t_1. The maximum marginal rate is equal to c. The condition in (12.3) that $k < 1$ ensures that the tax schedule is progressive; that is, the marginal tax rate increases as gross income increases, and the marginal rate exceeds the average rate. An increase in k implies that marginal tax rates increase more rapidly from t_1 (at the threshold income a_2) to their maximum of c.

The tax schedule specified above is therefore extremely flexible and is capable of describing a wide range of profiles of marginal and average tax rates. To give some idea of the extent to which it can approximate the complex schedule actually used in the UK, figure 12.1 illustrates the situation for the financial year 1977/78. The parameter values used are as follows: $a_1 = 2000$, $a_2 = 8000$, $k = 0.66$, $t_1 = 0.34$ and $c = 0.95$ (whence $h = 229.8$). Notice that it is necessary to use a value of c that is higher than the actual maximum marginal rate (of 0.83), since c is an asymptote and it is necessary to ensure that the profile has a marginal rate of 0.83 at appropriate income levels.

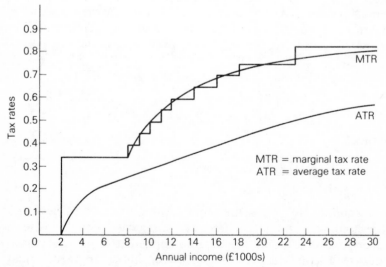

Figure 12.1   Average and marginal tax rates.

The tax schedule can be fitted to any actual schedule of marginal tax rates using ordinary least squares regression methods. Over the range $y > a_2$ the marginal rate of tax is given by

$$dT(y)/dy = c - (c - t_1)\{(1-k)(y/a_2)^{-k} + k(y/a_2)^{-1-k}\} \quad (12.4)$$

For a fixed k and a_2 (which is obtained directly from the actual schedule) a regression of the form $z = \alpha + \beta x$, where x is the term in curly brackets in (12.4), may be run. Results using different values of k may be compared to find the one that gives the best fit. For 1977/78 values (using the middle of each income range as the value of y, and with £30 000 as the maximum mid-point), the following result was obtained using data from Meade *et al.* (1978):

$$z = \quad 1.05 - 0.71x \qquad R^2 = 0.997 \qquad k = 0.5$$
$$(112.44)(-50.32)$$

Figures in parentheses are 't' values. This gives an asymptote of 1.05 and a 'standard rate' of 0.34 ($\beta = c - t_1$), and provides a very good fit. Different values of c and k were used for figure 12.1 as the line was not constrained to go through the mid-points of the ranges.

Total Income Tax Revenue

If the distribution function of before-tax income is denoted by $F(y)$, then total tax revenue per person, R, is given as

$$R = \int T(y) \, dF(y) \quad (12.5)$$

where integration is over the complete range of incomes $0 < y < \alpha$.

When the tax schedule (12.1) to (12.3) is substituted into the general expression (12.5) it can be seen that (as in chapter 11) a number of terms appear of the general form $\int^a y^r \, dF(y)$. Since by definition $\int y^r \, dF(y)$ is the rth moment about the origin, denoted μ'_r, the total revenue per head involves 'incomplete' moments (as integration is over a specified section of the income distribution). Simplification therefore requires the concept of the 'rth incomplete moment distribution function' of y, denoted $F_r(y)$ and defined as

$$F_r(y) = \int\limits^{y} u^r \, dF(u) \Big/ \int u^r \, dF(u) \quad (12.6)$$

This type of manipulation has already been examined in chapter 11, where it was found useful to introduce a general term $G(y)$, defined in equation (11.9). The present problem is slightly more cumbersome, and it is useful to generalize G somewhat by defining the function of two arguments, $G(r, y)$, using

$$G(r, y) = \mu'_r\{1 - F_r(y)\} - y\mu'_{r-1}\{1 - F_{r-1}(y)\} \qquad (12.7)$$

The term μ'_1 is the arithmetic mean, also denoted $\bar{y}$. This can be seen to involve the use of non-integer moment distribution functions $F_r(y)$. Although such functions are unusual, there are no new problems arising from their use. After some manipulation it can be found that

$$R = t_1\{G(1, a_1) - G(1, a_2)\} + cG(1, a_2) - hG(1 - k, a_2)$$

$$(12.8)$$

Total revenue per person is therefore a convenient function of just five parameters, c, a_1, a_2, t_1 and k, in addition to those required to describe the characteristics of the distribution of income. The values of these parameters are available for most tax systems, and although there is often a variety of threshold levels (depending on personal circumstances) it is not difficult to specify an appropriate value for the single threshold, a_1.

The expression for total revenue in (12.8) would serve little purpose if it were not possible to obtain convenient expressions for the various moment distributions $F_r(y)$, and moments μ'_r. Fortunately the properties of the lognormal distribution $\Lambda(\mu, \sigma^2)$ can be used, as described in chapter 11, since

$$\Lambda_r(\mu, \sigma^2) = \Lambda(\mu + r\sigma^2, \sigma^2) \qquad (12.9)$$

$$\mu'_r = \exp(r\mu + \tfrac{1}{2}r^2\sigma^2) \qquad (12.10)$$

where μ and σ^2 are the mean and variance of the logarithms of income.

12.2 Properties of Alternative Systems

Having set out the analytics of the tax model in the previous section, the built-in flexibility of various tax structures can now be examined. A useful feature of the model is that it can be used to examine the properties of tax parameters for a wide variation in average income. An equal proportionate increase in all incomes

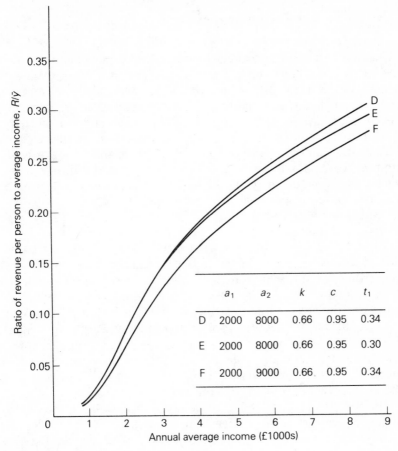

Figure 12.2 Total income tax revenue.

will change the mean of the logarithms of income, but will leave relative dispersion unchanged. The effect on total revenue of a general increase in incomes, with an unchanged tax schedule, can therefore be examined by considering variations in μ, with σ^2 unchanged. Comparisons among structures can also be made, in order to consider the implications of discretionary changes at different income levels. It is most convenient to illustrate the results diagrammatically, using the same simple computational method for evaluating the distribution function Λ as used in chapter 11.

Effective Average Tax Rates

It is useful to measure changes in total revenue per person, R, expressed as a ratio of average income, $\bar{y}$. This ratio may be called the effective average rate. Figure 12.2 provides three examples using equation (12.8), where it is assumed that σ^2 remains constant at 0.2. This roughly reflects the dispersion of male earnings over all age groups in the UK. The profile marked D in figure 12.2 corresponds to the tax schedule illustrated in figure 12.1. This profile can be seen to be sigmoid in shape, and asymptotically approaches a maximum rate of 0.95, which is the limiting case where all individuals pay the highest marginal rate. The section of the profile corresponding to low values of $\bar{y}$ relative to the threshold may be thought to be appropriate for a country with a very small direct tax base.

Figure 12.2 shows two further profiles. The effects of a reduction in the standard rate of tax to 0.30, and an increase in the level of income above which higher marginal rates are payable to £9000, are illustrated in profiles F and E respectively. Although all three profiles are sigmoid in shape, they become almost linear over a range of mean income from approximately £5000 to £9000. This arises because within that range a large proportion of incomes lie between a_1 and a_2 and are therefore subject to a constant marginal tax rate. As $\bar{y}$ rises further this effect will diminish, and the profiles will become more concave.

From these profiles it is not difficult to determine the extent of an inflation tax. An increase in money income due solely to inflation will lead to an increase in the effective average tax rate $(R/\bar{y})$ as a result of a movement along a particular profile. Constancy in the effective average tax rate can of course be maintained by increasing a_1 and a_2 by the same proportion as $\bar{y}$, so moving the profile to the right.

Effective Marginal Rates and Revenue Elasticities

This method of examining income tax revenues also allows direct calculation of the effective marginal tax rate (EMR), $dR/d\bar{y}$, and the elasticity of tax revenue with respect to mean income, $(dR/d\bar{y})(\bar{y}/R)$. These measures can be calculated for any tax structure or series of tax structures. This is an advantage of the present model, since previous studies of income tax elasticities apply to particular years only and have not examined the extent to which elasticities vary as average income increases, using an unchanged tax schedule.

Figure 12.3. shows elasticities and EMRs associated with the profiles in figure 12.2. As may be expected, the higher the elasticities, the lower the mean income level, while EMRs rise with mean income. Figure 12.3 shows clearly that the revenue elasticity schedule levels out at higher mean income levels, as a consequence of the 'standard rate' section in the tax function. However, the elasticity schedule will decline as mean income rises beyond £9000 (when more incomes become taxable at higher marginal rates). The effect of the standard rate on the EMR profiles is rather different. EMRs increase at a declining rate at mean income levels below about £5000. But the increase in EMRs is more uniform as $\bar{y}$ rises beyond this level. However the rate of increase will decline as mean income increases beyond £9000.

Finally it is interesting to note the effects of some parameter changes on elasticities and EMRs. Figure 12.3 shows that reducing the standard tax rate to 0.30 (profile E) increases the revenue elasticities and reduces the EMRs associated with each level of mean income. The effects are however greatest at higher mean incomes. Increasing the value of the parameter a_2 to £9000 (profile F) causes both elasticities and EMRs to decrease for each value of $\bar{y}$. It may also be seen that, unlike profile E, the decrease in the EMR compared with that for profile D is much greater at higher mean income levels.

Since the tax function in figure 12.1 from which profile D is derived approximates the UK in 1977/78, the results may be compared with estimates for the UK obtained by Hutton and Lambert (1980a). They found an elasticity of 1.78 and, although they do not present an estimate for the EMR, a value of 0.30 is implied (see Hutton and Lambert, 1980, p. 902). These estimates may be compared with values obtained from profile D at the appropriate mean income level of about £5000, where the elasticity and EMR are respectively 1.75 and 0.36. This simple method of modelling a complex tax system can thus produce sensible values for the measures commonly used to examine the built-in flexibility of tax systems. Furthermore the values are not very sensitive to changes in the dispersion of pre-tax incomes (as measured by σ^2), over the relevant range of average income. For example, when σ^2 takes the value of 0.15, the values of the revenue elasticity and effective marginal rate are respectively 1.72

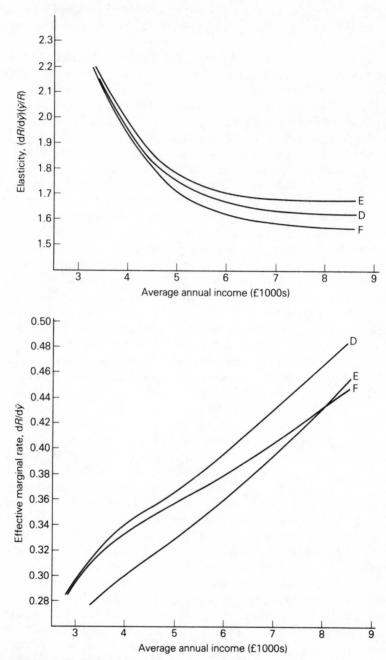

Figure 12.3   Elasticities and effective marginal rates.

and 0.359, at the mean income of £5039. The corresponding values for $\sigma^2 = 0.25$ are 1.75 and 0.378. There would of course be no difficulty in applying the above methods to a wide variety of tax parameters, income distribution parameters and rates of tax indexation.

Further Reading

This chapter is based on Creedy and Gemmell (1982). The tax function has been used in a larger analysis of the redistributive effects of taxes and transfers in Britain, including Value Added Tax, in Creedy and Gemmell (1984). The properties of alternative methods of indexation in the latter model are examined in Creedy and Gemmell (1985). A general analysis of built-in flexibility and income distribution in West Germany is contained in Spahn (1975). There are many studies of the built-in flexibility of particular systems, too numerous to mention here, but Dorrington (1974) discusses earlier British studies.

References

Adelman, I. G. (1958) A stochastic analysis of the size distribution of firms. *Journal of the American Statistical Association*, **53**, 893-904.

Aigner, D. J. and Goldberger, A. S. (1970) Estimation of Pareto's Law from grouped observations. *Journal of the American Statistical Association*, **65**, 712-23.

Aitchison, J. and Brown, J. A. C. (1954) On criteria for descriptions of income distribution. *Metroeconomica*, **6**, 88-107.

Aitchison, J. and Brown, J. A. C. (1957) *The Lognormal Distribution*. Cambridge: Cambridge University Press.

Atkinson, A. B. (1970) On the measurement of inequality. *Journal of Economic Theory*, **2**, 244-63.

Atkinson, A. B. (1983) *Social Justice and Public Policy*. Brighton: Wheatsheaf Books.

Atoda, N. and Tachibanaki, T. (1980) Earnings distribution and inequality over time. *Kyoto Institute of Economic Research Discussion Papers*, no. 144.

Barr, N. A., James, S. R. and Prest, A. R. (1977) *Self Assessment for Income Tax*. London: Heinemann.

Barriol, A. (1910) La valeur sociale d'un individu. *Review Economie Internationale*, December, 552-5.

Bartholomew, D. J. (1973) *Stochastic Models for Social Processes*. London: Wiley.

Becker, G. S. (1964) *Human Capital*. New York: National Bureau of Economic Research.

Benus, J. and Morgan, J. N. (1974) Time period, unit of analysis and income concept in the analysis of income distribution. In *The Personal Distribution of Income and Wealth* (ed. J. D. Smith), 209-29. New York: National Bureau of Economic Research.

Blaug, M. (1970) *An Introduction to the Economics of Education*. London: Penguin Education.

Blinder, A. S. (1974) *Towards an Economic Theory of Income Distribution.* Cambridge, Mass: MIT University Press.

Blomquist, N. S. (1981) The distribution of lifetime income: a case study of Sweden. In *The Statics and Dynamics of Income* (ed. N. A. Klevmarken and J. A. Lybeck), 105-33. Clevedon: Tieto.

Boag, H. (1916) Human capital and the cost of war. *Journal of the Royal Statistical Society,* **79**, 7-17.

Bosanquet, N. and Doeringer, P. D. (1973) Is there a dual labour market in Britain? *Economic Journal,* **83**, 421-35.

Boudon, R. (1973) *Mathematical Structures of Social Mobility.* New York: Elsevier.

Bowley, A. L. (1926) *Elements of Statistics.* London: P. S. King and Son.

Bowley, A. L. (1933) Frequency distributions of income, prices and other phenomena: A suggestion for study. *Econometrica,* **1**, 358-70.

Brown, J. A. C. (1967) The life cycle in income. Mimeo. University of Bristol.

Brown, J. A. C. (1976) The mathematical and statistical theory of income distribution. In *The Personal Distribution of Incomes* (ed. A. B. Atkinson), 72-97. London: George Allen and Unwin.

Cannan, E. (1914) *Wealth.* London: P. S. King and Son.

Champernowne, D. G. (1953) A model of income distribution. *Economic Journal,* **63**, 318-51.

Chesher, A. D. (1973).The observation of the law of proportionate growth. *University of Birmingham Discussion Paper,* Series A, No. 157.

Chesher, A. (1979) Testing the law of proportionate effect. *Journal of Industrial Economics,* **27**, 403-11.

Cheshire, P. C. and Stabler, M. J. (1976) Joint consumption benefits in recreational site 'surplus': an empirical estimate. *Regional Studies,* **10**.

Chisholm, A. H. (1971) A comparison of income averaging procedures for income tax purposes. *Australian Journal of Agricultural Economics,* **15**, 36-50.

Clark, H. F. (1937) *Life Earnings in Selected Occupations in the United States.* New York: Harper.

Cohen, A. I., Parnes, H. S. and Shea, J. R. (1974) Income instability among young and middle-aged men. In *The Personal Distribution of Income and Wealth* (ed. J. D. Smith), 151-218. New York: National Bureau of Economic Research.

Colwyn, Lord (Chairman) (1920) *Report of the Royal Commission on the Income Tax.* London: HMSO, Cmnd 615.

Cowell, F. A. (1975) On the estimation of a lifetime income – a correction. *Journal of American Statistical Association,* **70**, 588-9.

Cramer, H. (1946) *Mathematical Methods of Statistics.* Princeton: Princeton University Press.

Crammond, E. (1915) The cost of war. *Journal of the Royal Statistical Society,* **78**, 361-99.

Creedy, J. (1972) Economic Cycles in the Lives of Individuals and Families. B.Phil. Thesis, Oxford.

158   References

Creedy, J. (1973) A problem in the estimation of double-log Engel curves. *Oxford Bulletin of Economics and Statistics*, **35**, 217-22.

Creedy, J. (1974) Income changes over the life cycle. *Oxford Economic Papers*, **26**, 405-23.

Creedy, J. (1974a) The chemist's earnings – past and present. *Chemistry in Britain*, **10**, 50-3.

Creedy, J. (1974b) Inter-regional mobility: a cross-section analysis. *Scottish Journal of Political Economy*, **21**, 41-53.

Creedy, J. (1975) Aggregation and the distribution of income. *Oxford Bulletin of Economics and Statistics*, **37**, 91-101.

Creedy, J. (1975a) Year-to-year changes in chemists' earnings. *Chemistry in Britain*, **11**, 140-3.

Creedy, J. (1975b) Income concept, time period and changes in earnings. *University of Reading Discussion Papers in Economics, Series A*, no. 76.

Creedy, J. (1975c) Expectations and the variability of earnings. *University of Reading Discussion Papers in Economics, Series A*, no. 72.

Creedy, J. (1977) The distribution of lifetime earnings. *Oxford Economic Papers*, **29**, 412-29.

Creedy, J. (1977a) The principle of transfers and the variance of logarithms. *Oxford Bulletin of Economics and Statistics*, **39**, 152-8.

Creedy, J. (1977b) Pareto and the distribution of income. *Review of Income and Wealth*, **23**, 405-11.

Creedy, J. (1977c) Earnings in an hierarchical structure. *University of Reading Discussion Papers in Economics, Series A*, no. 92.

Creedy, J. (1978) A note on the analysis of changes in earnings. *Economic Journal*, **88**, 126-33.

Creedy, J. (1978a) Negative income taxes and income redistribution. *Oxford Bulletin of Economics and Statistics*, **40**, 363-9.

Creedy, J. (1979) The inequality of earnings and the accounting period. *Scottish Journal of Political Economy*, **26**, 89-96.

Creedy, J. (1979a) Income averaging and progressive taxation. *Journal of Public Economics*, **12**, 387-97.

Creedy, J. (1980) The new government pension scheme: A simulation analysis. *Oxford Bulletin of Economics and Statistics*, **42**, 51-64.

Creedy, J. (1980a) Pension schemes and the limits to redistribution: some policy alternatives. In *Income Distribution: The Limits to Redistribution* (ed. D. Collard, R. Lecomber and M. Slater), 103-18. Bristol: Scientechnica for the Colston Research Society.

Creedy, J. (1981) Taxation and national insurance contributions in Britain. *Journal of Public Economics*, **15**, 379-88.

Creedy, J. (1982) The changing burden of national insurance contributions and income taxation in Britain. *Scottish Journal of Political Economy*, **29**, 127-38.

Creedy, J. (1982a) The British state pension: Contributions, benefits and indexation. *Oxford Bulletin of Economics and Statistics*, **44**, 97-112.

Creedy, J. (1982b) Some analytics of income tax/transfer schemes. *Journal of Economic Studies*, **9**, 30-9.

Creedy, J. (1982c) *State Pensions in Britain*. Cambridge: Cambridge University Press.

Creedy, J. and Disney, R. (1981) Changes in labour market states in Great Britain. *Scottish Journal of Political Economy*, **28**, 76-85.

Creedy, J. and Disney, R. (1981a) Eligibility for unemployment benefits in Britain. *Oxford University Papers*, **33**, 256-73.

Creedy, J. and Disney, R. (1985) *Social Insurance in Transition: An Economic Analysis*. Oxford: Oxford University Press.

Creedy, J. and Gemmell, N. (1982) The built-in flexibility of progressive income taxes: a simple model. *Public Finance*, **37**, 361-72.

Creedy. J. and Gemmell, N. (1984) Income redistribution through taxes and transfers in Britain. *Scottish Journal of Political Economy*, **31**, 44-59.

Creedy, J. and Gemmell, N. (1985) The indexation of taxes and transfers in Britain. *Manchester School* (in press).

Creedy, J. and Hart, P. E. (1979) Age and the distribution of earnings. *Economic Journal*, **89**, 280-93.

Creedy, J., Hart, P. E., Jonsson, A. and Klevmarken, N. A. (1981) The distribution of cohort incomes in Sweden 1960-73: A comparative static analysis. In *The Statics and Dynamics of Income* (ed. N. A. Klevmarken and J. A. Lybeck), pp. 55-80. Clevedon: Tieto.

Creedy, J., Hart, P. E. and Klevmarken, N. A. (1981) Income mobility in Great Britain and Sweden. In *The Statics and Dynamics of Income* (ed. N. A. Klevmarken and J. A. Lybeck), pp. 195-211. Clevedon: Tieto.

Dalton, H. (1929) *Some Aspects of the Inequality of Incomes in Modern Communities*. London: George Routledge and Sons.

Dalton, H. (1954) *Principles of Public Finance*, 4th edn. London: Routledge and Kegan Paul.

Dasgupta, P., Sen, A. and Starrett, D. (1973) Notes on the measurement of inequality. *Journal of Economic Theory*, **6**, 180-7.

David, M. et al. (1969) The operation of the 1964 averaging provisions of the internal revenue code: a simulation study and recommended changes. *University of Wisconsin Social Systems Research Institute*.

Department of Education and Science (1971) *Statistics of Education*. Special Series No. 3. London: HMSO.

Department of Employment (1973) Low pay and changes in earnings. *Employment Gazette*, April, pp. 335-48.

Department of Employment (1977) How individual people's earnings change. *Employment Gazette*, January, pp. 19-24.

Dorrington, J. C. (1974) A structural approach to estimating the built-in flexibility of United Kingdom taxes on personal incomes. *Economic Journal*, **84**, 576-94.

Dublin, L. I. and Lotka, A. J. (1930) *The Money Value of a Man*. New York: Ronald Press.

Edgeworth, F. Y. (1925) *Papers Relating to Political Economy*, Vol. II. London: Macmillan.

Farr, W. (1853) The income and property tax. *Journal of the Royal Statistical Society*, **16**, 1-14.

Fase, M. M. G. (1970) *An Econometric Model of Age-Income Profiles*. Rotterdam: Rotterdam University Press.

Fase, M. M. G. (1971) On the estimation of lifetime income. *Journal of the American Statistical Association*, **66**, 686-92.

Fisher, J. (1952) Income, spending and saving patterns of consumer units in different age groups. In *Studies in Income and Wealth*, Vol. 15 (ed. E. D. Hollander), pp. 75-102. New York: National Bureau of Economic Research.

Friedman, M. (1957) *A Theory of the Consumption Function*. Princeton: Princeton University Press.

Friedman, M. and Kuznets, S. (1945) *Income from Independent Professional Practice*. New York: National Bureau of Economic Research.

Friesen, P. H. and Miller, D. (1983) Annual inequality and lifetime inequality. *Quarterly Journal of Economics*, **98**, 139-55.

Galton, F. (1889) *Natural Inheritance*. London: Macmillan.

Gibrat, R. (1931) *Les Inegalites Economiques*. Paris: Sirey.

Giffen, R. (1880) *Essays in Finance*. London: G. Bell and Sons.

Goldberger, A. S. (1964) *Econometric Theory*. Chichester: Wiley.

Goodman, L. A. (1961) Statistical methods for the mover-stayer model. *Journal of the American Statistical Association*, 56, 841-68.

Haldane, J. B. S. (1942) Moments of the distribution of powers and products of normal variates. *Biometrika*, **33**, 226-42.

Hamdan, M. A. (1971) The logarithm of the sum of two correlated lognormal variates. *Journal of the American Statistical Association*, **66**, 105-106.

Hanna, F. A. (1948) The accounting period and the distribution of income. In *Analysis of Wisconsin Income* (ed. F. A. Hanna, J. A. Pechman and S. M. Lerner). New York: National Bureau of Economic Research.

Hart, P. E. (1962) The size and growth of firms. *Economica*, **24**, 29-39.

Hart, P. E. (1968) Comment on a paper by A. R. Thatcher. *Journal of the Royal Statistical Society, Series A*, **131**, 181.

Hart, P. E. (1973). Random processes and economic size distributions. Mimeo. University of Reading.

Hart, P. E. (1974) Changes in earnings and regression bias. *University of Reading Discussion Papers in Economics, Series A*, no. 63.

Hart, P. E. (1975) Moment distributions in economics – an exposition. *Journal of the Royal Statistical Society, Series A*, **138**, 423-34.

Hart, P. E. (1976) The dynamics of earnings, 1963-1973. *Economic Journal*, **86**, 541-65.

Hart, P. E. (1976a) The comparative statics and dynamics of income distributions. *Journal of the Royal Statistical Society, Series A*, **137**, 108-25.

Hart, P. E. (1978) Redundant inequalities. *National Institute of Economic and Social Research Discussion Paper*, no. 18.

Hart, P. E. (1980) Lognormality and the principle of transfers. *Oxford Bulletin of Economics and Statistics*, **42**, 263-8.

Hart, P. E. (1981) The statics and dynamics of income distributions: a survey.

References 161

In *The Statics and Dynamics of Income* (ed. N. A. Klevmarken and J. A. Lybeck), pp. 1-22. Clevedon: Tieto.

Hart, P. E. (1982) The sizes and growths of trade unions. *University of Reading Discussion Paper in Economics, Series A*, no. 128.

Hart, P. E. (1982a) Entropy, moments and aggregate business concentration in the U.K. *Oxford Bullein of Economics and Statistics*, **44**, 113-26.

Hart, P. E. (1983) The size mobility of earnings. *Oxford Bulletin of Economics and Statistics*, **45**, 181-94.

Hart, P. E. and Prais, S. J. (1956) The analysis of business concentration: a statistical approach. *Journal of the Royal Statistical Society, Series A*, **119**, 150-81.

Hinkley, D. V. and Revankar, N. S. (1977) Estimation of the Pareto Law from under-reported data: a further analysis. *Journal of Econometrics*, **5**, 1-11.

Hull, C. R. (ed.) (1899) *The Economic Writings of Sir William Petty*. Cambridge: Cambridge University Press.

Hutton, J. P. and Lambert, P. J. (1980) Evaluating income tax revenue elasticities. *Economic Journal*, **90**, 901-6.

Hutton, J. P. and Lambert, P. J. (1980a) Income tax, inflation tax, and the tax elasticity: a model for the U.K. *York Institute of Social and Economic Research Discussion Paper*, no. 59.

Irvine, I. J. (1981) The use of cross-section microdata in life cycle models: an application to inequality theory in nonstationary economies. *Quarterly Journal of Economics*, **96**, 301-16.

Johnson, N. L. and Kotz, S. (1970) *Distributions in Statistics: Continuous Univariate Distributions, I*. Boston: Houghton Mifflin.

Jöreskog, K. G. (1978) An econometric model for multivariate panel data. *Annales de l'Insee*, **30**, 335-66.

Kalecki, M. (1946) On the Gibrat distribution. *Econometrica*, **13**, 161-70.

Kesselman, J. R. (1982) Deferral, indexation, and averaging of taxes: thoughts on the 1981 Federal budget and future policy options. *Canadian Tax Journal*, **30**, 360-88.

Kiker, B. F. (1966) The historical roots of the concept of human capital. *Journal of Political Economy*, **74**, 481-99.

Kiker, B. F. and Cochrane, J. L. (1973) War and human capital in western economic analysis. *History of Political Economy*, **5**, 375-98.

Klein, L. R. (1962) *An Introduction to Econometrics*. Englewood Cliffs: Prentice Hall.

Kravis, I. (1962) *The Structure of Income*. Pennsylvania: University of Pennsylvania.

Krelle, W. H. and Shorrocks, A. F. (eds) (1978) *Personal Income Distribution*. Amsterdam: North-Holland.

Kuznets, S. (1950) *Shares of Upper Income Groups in Income and Savings*. New York: National Bureau of Economic Research.

Lillard, L. A. and Weiss, Y. (1979) Components of variation in panel earnings data: American scientists 1960-1970. *Econometrica*, **47**, pp. 437-54.

Lillard, L. A. and Willis, R. J. (1978) Dynamic aspects of earning mobility. *Econometrica*, 46, 985-1012.

Lipson, E. (1949) *The Economic History of England: Vol. I. The Middle Ages*. London: A. and C. Black.

Long, J. S. (1983) *Confirmatory Factor Analysis*. Beverly Hills: Sage.

Long, J. S. (1983a) *Covariance Structure Models*. Beverly Hills: Sage.

Lydall, H. F. (1955) The life cycle in income, saving and asset ownership. *Econometrica*, 23, 131-50.

Lydall, H. F. (1955a) *British Incomes and Savings*. Oxford: Basil Blackwell.

Lydall, H. F. (1968) *The Structure of Earnings*. Oxford: Clarendon Press.

Macaulay, F. R. (1922) Pareto's Law and the general problems of mathematically describing the frequency distribution of income and wealth. In *Income in the United States: Its Amount and Distribution* (ed. W. C. Mitchell), pp. 344-94. New York: National Bureau of Economic Research.

Malinvaud, E. (1970) *Statistical Methods of Econometrics*. Amsterdam: North-Holland.

Mandelbrot, V. (1960) The Pareto-Levy law and the distribution of income. *International Economic Review*, 1, 79-106.

Marfels, C. (1972) On testing concentration measures. *Zeitschrift für Nationalokonomie*, 32, 461-86.

Markandya, A. (1982) The measurement of earnings mobility among occupational groups. *Scottish Journal of Political Economy*, 29, 75-88.

Marshall, A. (1890) *Principles of Economics*. London: Macmillan.

McCall, J. J. (1971) A Markovian model of income dynamics. *Journal of the American Statistical Association*, 66, 439-47.

Meade, J. E. *et al.* (1978) *The Structure and Reform of Direct Taxation*. London: Allen and Unwin.

Merkies, A. H. Q. M. (1968) On an optimal use of the income averaging facilities in the proposals of the Carter Commission. *Canadian Journal of Economics*, 3, 255-67.

Merrett, S. (1966) The rate of return to education: a critique. *Oxford Economic Papers*, 18, 289-303.

Mill, J. S. (1848) *Principles of Political Economy*. London: J. W. Parker.

Mincer, J. (1970) Distribution of labour incomes: a survey. *Journal of Economic Literature*, 8, 1-26.

Mookherjee, D. and Shorrocks, A. F. (1982) A decomposition analysis of the trend in U.K. Income inequality. *Economic Journal*, 92, 886-902.

Morgan, J. (1962) The anatomy of income distribution. *Review of Economics and Statistics*, 44, 270-83.

Moss, M. (1979) Income distribution issues viewed in a lifetime income perspective. *Review of Income and Wealth*, 25, 119-36.

Nicholson, J. S. (1891) The living capital of the United Kingdom. *Economic Journal*, 1, 95-107.

Ord, J. K. (1975) Statistical models for personal income distributions. In *Statistical Distributions in Scientific Work* (ed. G. P. Patil, S. Kotz and J. K. Ord), 151-8. New York: Reidel.

Pareto, V. (1896) *La Courbe de la Repartition de la Richesse*. Universite de Lausanne.

Pareto, V. (1897) *Cours d'Economie Politique*.

Pareto, V. (1906) Determination mathematique des resultats des experience. Reprinted in Volume 8 of *Oeuvres Complete* (ed. G. Busino).

Pareto, V. (1909) *Manuel d'Economie Politique*.

Pigou, A. C. (1952) *The Economics of Welfare*. London: Macmillan.

Polinsky, A. M. (1974) Imperfect capital markets, intertemporal redistribution and progressive taxation. In *Redistribution Through Public Choice* (ed. H. M. Hochman and G. E. Peterson), pp. 229-58. New York: Columbia University Press.

Prais, S. J. (1955) Measuring social mobility. *Journal of the Royal Statistical Society, Series A*, 118, 56-66.

Prest, A. R. and Stark, T. (1967) *Some Aspects of Income Distribution in the U.K. Since World War II*. Manchester: Manchester Statistical Society.

Radcliffe, Lord (Chairman) (1955) *Report of the Royal Commission on the Taxation of Profits and Incomes*. London: HMSO, Cmnd 9474.

Rothschild, M. and Stiglitz, J. E. (1971) Increasing risk II: its economic consequences. *Journal of Economic Theory*, 3, 66-84.

Rowntree, B. S. (1899) *Poverty: A Study in Town Life*.

Royal Commission on the Distribution of Income and Wealth (1975) *Report no. 1. Initial Report on the Standarding Reference*. London: HMSO, Cmnd 6171.

Royal Commission on the Distribution of Income and Wealth (1976) *Report no. 3. Higher Incomes from Employment*. London: HMSO, Cmnd 6383.

Royal Commission on Doctors' and Dentists' Remuneration (1960) *Supplement to Report: Further Statistical Appendix*. London: HMSO, Cmnd 1064.

Rutherford, R. S. G. (1955) Income distribution: a new model. *Econometrica*, 23, 277-94.

Salant, S. W. (1977) Search theory and duration: a theory of sorts. *Quarterly Journal of Economics*, 91, 39-57.

Salem, A. Z. B. and Mount, T. D. (1974) A convenient descriptive model of income distribution: the gamma density. *Econometrica*, 42, 1115-27.

Schumpeter, J. (1968) *Ten Great Economists*. London: Allen and Unwin.

Sen, A. K. (1973) *On Economic Inequality*. Oxford: Clarendon Press.

Shorrocks, A. F. (1975) On stochastic models of size distribution. *Review of Economic Studies*, 42, 631-41.

Shorrocks, A. F. (1976) Income mobility and the Markov assumption. *Economic Journal*, 86, 566-78.

Shorrocks, A. F. (1978) The measurement of mobility. *Econometrica*, 46, 1013-24.

Shorrocks, A. F. (1978a) Income inequality and income mobility. *Journal of Economic Theory*, 19, 376-93.

Shorrocks, A. F. (1981) Income stability in the United States. In *The Statics and Dynamics of Income* (ed. N. A. Klevmarken and J. A. Lybeck), 175-94. Clevedon: Tieto.

Simons, H. (1938) *Personal Income Taxation.* Chicago: Chicago University Press.

Singer, B. and Spilerman, S. (1974) Social mobility models for heterogeneous populations. In *Sociological Methodology* (ed. H. L. Costner), pp. 356-401. San Francisco: Jussey-Bass.

Singer, B. and Spilerman, S. (1976) The representation of social processes by Markov models. *American Journal of Sociology*, **82**, 1-54.

Singh, S. K. and Maddala, G. S. (1976) A function for size distribution of incomes. *Econometrica*, **44**, 963-70.

Smith, A. (1776) *The Wealth of Nations.* London: Strahan and Cadell.

Spahn, P. B. (1975) Simulating long-term changes of income distribution within an income tax model for West Germany. *Public Finance*, **30**, 231-50.

Spencer, H. (1897) *Principles of Ethics* (reprinted 1978). Indianapolis: Liberty Classics.

Steger, W. A. (1956) Averaging income for tax purposes: a statistical study. *National Tax Journal*, **9**, 97-115.

Steinberg, E. (1977) Measuring income inequality with extended earnings periods. *Monthly Labour Review*, June.

Steindl, J. (1965) *Random Processes and the Growth of Firms: A study of the Pareto Law.* London: Griffin.

Stone, J. R. N. (1973) A system of social matrices. *Review of Income and Wealth*, **10**, 143-66.

Thatcher, A. R. (1971) Year-to-year variations in the earnings of individuals. *Journal of the Royal Statistical Society, Series A*, **134**, 374-82.

Tibbetts, F. C. (1940) The accounting period in federal income taxation. *Southern Economic Journal*, **7**, 362-79.

Tuck, R. H. (1954) *An Essay on the Economic Theory of Rank.* Oxford: Basil Blackwell.

Vandome, P, (1958) Aspects of the dynamics of consumer behaviour. *Oxford Bulletin of Economics and Statistics*, **20**, 65-105.

Vickrey, W. (1938) Averaging of income for income tax purposes. *Journal of Political Economy*, **47**, 379-97.

Weisbrod, B. A. (1962) An expected income measure of economic welfare. *Journal of Political Economy*, **70**, 355-67.

Weiss, Y. (1972) The risk element in occupational and educational choice. *Journal of Political Economy*, **80**, 1203-13.

Wharton School of Finance and Commerce (1957) *Study of Consumer Expenditure, Income and Savings.* Pennsylvania: University of Pennsylvania.

Wilkinson, B. W. (1966) Present values of lifetime earnings in different occupations. *Journal of Political Economy*, **74**, 556-72.

Wold, J. O. and Whittle, P. (1957) A model explaining the Pareto distribution of wealth. *Econometrica*, **25**, 591-5.

Woytinsky, W. S. (1943) *Earnings and Social Security in the United States.*

Index

168   *Index*

Singh, S. K., 7
Smith, Adam, 78
social class, 49
Social Darwinists, 23
social dividend schemes, 132–8
social insurance contributions, 3,
 131, 138
social mobility, 59
solicitors, 111
Spahn, P. B., 155
Spencer, H., 23
Spilerman, S., 57
Stabler, M. J., 27. 30
Stamp, Josiah, 22, 30
Starrett, D., 13
Stark, T., 43, 98
Steger, W. A., 130
Steinberg, E., 98
Steindl, J., 22, 30
Stiglitz, J. E., 130
stochastic models, 5–6, 22, 23, 59,
 77, 84–5
stochastic processes, 4–5, 7, 22, 30,
 33, 65, 80
Stone, J. R. N., 59
surveyors, 109, 111
Sweden, 43–7, 74, 83
Sylvester's formula, 58

Tachibanaki, T., 118
Taylor expansion, 17
Taylor series, 15
'temporary' income, 34, 121
Thatcher, A. R., 42, 43, 66
Tibbetts, F. C., 130
time
 effects, 6, 71, 76
 models: continuous, 49, 51, 56–8;
  discrete, 51, 57

periods, 2, 33, 34, 38, 40, 41, 44,
 52, 71, 97–105
profiles, 111
series data, 40, 42
series models, 3, 40
trade unions, 21
transfers, 4, 6
 inter-regional, 18
 perverse, 18
 Principle of, 11–21
 and taxation, 131–45, 155
transition matrices, 49–51
transition probabilities, 50, 51, 56,
 57, 58
Tuck, R. H., 30

unemployment, 3, 27, 40, 44, 49, 73
United Kingdom, 43–7, 85, 92–3,
 98–100, 122, 125–30, 139,
 140, 146, 153
United States, 43–7, 98, 108, 122
university teachers, 111
utility, 11, 12, 78, 124

Value Added Tax, 155
value of man, 107, 118
Vickrey, W., 122

wealth, 1, 117
Weiss, Y., 48, 78, 79
welfare, 11, 12, 13, 14
West Germany, 155
Whittle, P., 30
Wilkinson, B. W., 118
Willis, R. J., 48
Wisconsin, 122
Wold, J. O., 30
Woytinsky, W. S., 68